Creating a Small Business Cybersecurity Program

Alan Watkins

Copyright © 2020 CISO DRG

Creating a Small Business Cybersecurity Program

To contact the authors, write the publisher at the address provided above, "Attention: Author Services."

Edited by Bill Bonney
Artwork by Gwendolyn Peres
Formatting by Last Mile Publishing

Dedication

I dedicate this book to my dear friend and cybersecurity evangelist, Liz Fraumann. For her inspiration and commitment to bringing cybersecurity awareness to the community, especially small businesses, and also to her passion for high school and middle school students to learn cybersecurity skills. It was an honor and my pleasure to help her create Securing Our eCITY in San Diego, providing a national benefit through the collaboration of regional experts sharing their skills and expertise.

Acknowledgments

I want to acknowledge the following people for their contributions, directly or indirectly, in giving me encouragement, providing resource materials or assistance with proofreading the manuscript, and otherwise gave me inspiration to focus on supporting small businesses:

First, to the *CISO Desk Reference* team –

Bill Bonney – for providing assistance and guidance in getting this book off the drawing board and into publication, including providing editorial comments and suggestions.

Gary Hayslip – for providing inspiration to write this book; for setting the bar high in sharing his knowledge and experience to help others achieve their goals.

Matt Stamper – for providing insights into integrating privacy requirements with cybersecurity; for helping me to learn new aspects of federal consumer rights laws; for letting me discover that the basics of consumer privacy rights go so far beyond cybersecurity.

And, to some of my former colleagues and business associates:

Mike Davis – for all of those times when we reviewed each other's presentations and other documents, especially the ones related to risk assessments.

Tony Krzyzewski – for the discussions to focus on small businesses for implementing the CIS Controls.

Special Agent **Parker Scott**, San Diego InfraGard Members Alliance; **Liz Fraumann**, Securing Our eCITY; **Rusty Sailors**; **Macy Dennis**; and many others from the San Diego cybersecurity community.

Copyrights and Licenses

This book contains references to products and materials created and owned by other entities, which are covered under one or more laws or regulations related to registered trademarks, service marks, copyrights or Creative Commons licensing. Where the content has been annotated to indicate the owner of the materials, such entity still maintains its rights of ownership to the respective content under applicable laws and regulations. Inclusion or use of references in this book to any products or services are provided for informational purposes only and do not constitute an endorsement of any particular company, product or service; except in the case of the CIS Controls®, which the author does endorse and support.

This book specifically describes sections of the CIS Controls®, which is licensed under the:

Creative Commons *Attribution* | *Non-Commercial* | *No Derivatives v.4.0 International Public License*

found at:

https://creativecommons.org/licenses/by-nc-nd/4.0/legalcode)

In addition, the book discusses the CIS® Risk Assessment Method (CIS RAM), which is also covered under the Creative Commons license. Use of the materials is granted to the author by Center for Internet Security, Inc. (CIS®) through a CIS Controls Supporter License Agreement, as amended, which allows rearranging of the Controls and redistribution; provided, however, that users of this material, as part of the CIS Controls framework, are directed to the original set of Controls as published by CIS, located at http://www.cisecurity.org/controls/. As an extension of the Creative Commons license, you are authorized to copy and redistribute the

CIS Controls content as a framework for use by you, within your organization for non-commercial purposes only, provided that (i) appropriate credit is given to CIS, and (ii) a link to the license is provided, as well as the link to the original CIS Controls. You may not remix, transform or build upon these materials (for the CIS Controls), or distribute them in any way, without prior written approval from CIS.

> The Center for Internet Security, Inc. (CIS®) is a 501c3 non-profit organization whose mission is to identify, develop, validate, promote, and sustain best practices in cybersecurity; deliver world-class cybersecurity solutions to prevent and rapidly respond to cyber incidents; and build and lead communities to enable an environment of trust in cyberspace. For additional information, go to https://www.cisecurity.org/

Table of Contents

For decades, there have been people who claim to be information technology (IT) and security experts who have been proponents of using FUD (fear, uncertainty, and doubt) to pressure businesses into using certain products or services to "keep them safe from cyber-attacks." These tactics cause significant distrust by small business owners of the doomsayers' proposed solutions and immobilize us rather than spurring us on. The goal of this book is to discuss the realities of cybersecurity and small businesses, using a business risk perspective, and focusing on helping small businesses be successful at managing cyber risks.

Who should read this book?

How do we define a "small business?" The U.S. Small Business Administration defines it as having less than 500 employees. This book is best for businesses with 50 or more employees who are either creating their first cybersecurity plan or formalizing a collection of plans and procedures that grew organically as the business grew. Hopefully, this is a natural progression for the firm. If the need comes from a recent incident or audit finding, we recognize you're under a bit more pressure right now, and we're glad you found this book and are confident that the practical, hands-on guidance will help you get your program in place quickly.

Two additional books in the CISO Desk Reference Guide Small Business Series include *Be Your Own CISO*, best for smaller companies where the owner is providing direction on security and *The Essential Guide to Cybersecurity for SMBs*, which provides a strategic view for companies wishing to mature their cybersecurity programs.

The point of writing this book is to provide practical actions that small business owners can take at minimal cost to protect their business operations and any sensitive or confidential information under their control. In addition, Appendix B provides references to several free and publicly available resources to make it as easy as possible to implement a cybersecurity program in a small business with limited financial and human resources.

One of the goals of this book is to enable non-technical business owners and their employees to define and implement a workable cybersecurity program that fits within the current culture of your small business. Information technology should be a business enabler and cybersecurity should support the technology infrastructure and protect information assets, as an enabler of business risk management.

If you think about creating and implementing a cybersecurity program, it would generally include the basic phases shown in Figure I-1 below. This book primarily covers the first two phases, while providing an overview of implementing security control measures indicated in the third phase.

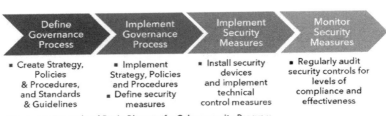

Figure I-1. *Example of Basic Phases of a Cybersecurity Program*

This book does not provide step-by-step instructions for configuring specific devices or setting up ongoing monitoring. For that level of detail, you should look for instruction manuals for the systems you have purchased and the applications you use.

Responding properly to cyber threats and risks may take some specialized skills to implement some of the necessary technical security solutions. However, the methods and actions recommended in this book take into account that many small businesses simply don't have staff who are skilled in cybersecurity. While some of the technical terminology cannot be completely removed, this book describes cybersecurity principles and tasks in common business language. This should help make it easier and more cost-effective for you to work with cybersecurity experts, and hopefully, for you to become a more educated consumer. That is not to say that you won't need to have someone with basic technology skills to help with the installation and configuration of certain devices, depending on what you choose to implement.

What should you expect from this book?

As you probably know, technology books can be filled with technical terms and lots of acronyms. This book intentionally stays away from technical language; however, the following acronyms and abbreviations are used in various chapters and commonly found in other sources. They are defined here for easy reference, in addition to the glossary in Appendix A. You may also find a few other acronyms used just once and defined where they are used.

- BCP – Business Continuity Plan
- CCPA – California Consumer Privacy Act
- CSP – Cloud Service Provider
- DRP – Disaster Recovery Plan
- FTC – Federal Trade Commission (U.S. Department of Commerce)
- GDPR – General Data Protection Regulation (European)
- ISP – Internet Service Provider
- PCI-DSS – Payment Card Industry Data Security Standards
- RMP – Risk Management Plan
- SMB – Small/Medium Business

Do you need to review every chapter of this book? Not necessarily, although it would probably be helpful. The book is designed as a bootstrap for small business owners who are just getting started and therefore opens with some basic principles and guidelines for creating a core set of business governance documents. If you have been operating your business for a while, you may want to skim over those early sections of the book and focus on the topics that are new to you. At the end of each chapter, you will find a summary of "Key Points" and a few "Recommended Action Items" related to the chapter topic to help guide you down the path toward creating a successful cybersecurity program.

We will start with how to incorporate cybersecurity into your governance documents, followed by a chapter covering risk management. Then we provide an overview of the key components in a small business cybersecurity program and describe the cybersecurity lifecycle process. There is a chapter to help you understand how privacy requirements relate to security controls. The concluding chapters provide simple steps for creating a basic cybersecurity program for your small business – at minimal cost – as well as how to begin implementation. The book includes ready-to-use templates for most of the recommended business documents. These should help spur your thoughts as you begin creating customized documents specifically for your small business. Of course, you should only take what you want to use – what makes sense for you and fits in with your business goals and operations.

You are probably well aware that nothing in life is actually free. However, this book provides many recommendations that have a minimal cost, which generally involve policies and procedures. This means there shouldn't be a direct expense to create them. On the other hand, implementing some of the security measures defined in the policies and procedures may involve purchasing certain devices or software, as well as conducting some training for your employees. In certain cases, hiring an expert to install and configure security devices may be necessary. The recommendations focus on low-cost options and provide methods for prioritizing what controls or security measures should be implemented in a phased approach over time. Each small business owner should balance the estimated costs against the potential loss or damage resulting from a cyberattack. Decisions should be based on a business risk assessment, not solely on recommendations from this book.

At the end of the book, you will find Appendix A, a Glossary of Terms used to describe various aspects of cybersecurity. This includes terms beyond those that are used in this book, which you might hear from contractors, vendors, or technology professionals. It is intended as a ready reference to help you understand what some of those folks are trying to explain. This book is just a starting point for your small business and for you to begin building a culture of cybersecurity awareness within your business. To that end, Appendix B contains a list of references and resources that are publicly available, where you can get additional information. Most of them are government agencies, but there are also some non-profits as well as a few private companies. Next, Appendix C provides more details and steps you can take to incorporate cyber risks into your business risk management plan. Finally, Appendix D contains example documents and templates.

Now that you know what to expect from this book, let's start by reviewing some recent statistics for small businesses and continue with basic business governance.

Cybersecurity and the Small Business

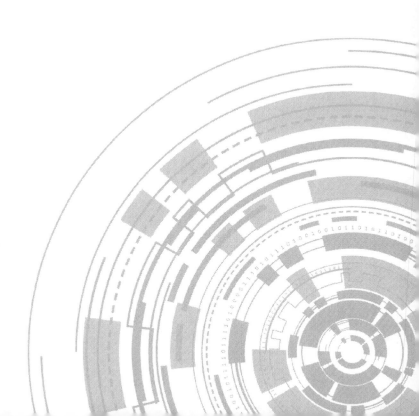

Chapter 1

The Objective is Cyber Resilience

We've all heard that being the victim of a cyberattack is a matter of **when** and not **if**. One report, from Hiscox Insurance, found that 47% of small businesses were victims of cyberattacks in 2019 (up from 33% in 2018) and estimates the annual cost of cyberattacks to be approximately $14,000 per incident for very small businesses (micro SMBs – less than 50 employees).[1] Another report, the Verizon 2019 Data Breach Investigations Report, found that 43% of more than 17,000 global data breaches targeted small businesses having less than 250 employees, with an average loss of $7,611 per incident.[2] This is not intended to take us down the FUD rabbit hole. It is meant to point out that small businesses have been and will remain targets of cyberattacks. This is primarily due to a lack of sufficient security measures, or what is called "cyber hygiene," at many small businesses.

So, why should you be concerned with cyberattacks on your small business? Because most aspects of businesses today rely on technology (computer systems and networks, tablets, and smartphones) for basic operations and functions. Furthermore, those cyberattacks don't have to target your computer systems directly. They could disrupt or damage your suppliers or vendors, partner companies, financial institutions, distribution channels, your Internet Service Provider (ISP) or Cloud Service Provider (CSP), or the utilities and city services upon which rely. Viewing cybersecurity as part of

---

[1] 2019 Hiscox Cyber Readiness Report
    https://www.hiscox.com/documents/2019-Hiscox-Cyber-Readiness-Report.pdf

[2] Verizon 2019 Data Breach Investigations Report
    https://enterprise.verizon.com/resources/reports/dbir/

business risk management is simply a prudent decision to maintain the health and growth of your business.

This book provides you with a way to develop a plan of action for creating a cybersecurity program at minimal cost to the business. By the end of this book, I hope that you end up with the necessary documents to incorporate into your business plan and meet your business goals and objectives. The resulting program should allow you to implement adequate security measures with minimal impact on your small business operations.

Many businesses consider their IT and cybersecurity functions to be cost centers – which is true; they are not revenue centers. However, those businesses sometimes forget to factor in the benefits those functions can bring. One beneficial aspect is having increased resilience in the computing environment. This makes it easier to respond to and recover from a cyberattack, or even from other disasters which impact computer systems. Another potential benefit of the costs for some security measures is that they are highly scalable – the same expenditure to protect the confidential information of 100 customers may also protect one million customers.

When completing a thorough cost-benefit analysis, the expense to implement and maintain cybersecurity systems and procedures should be factored into the cost of doing business. This is the same as accounting for expenses related to office space leasing, utilities, and insurance. Then, the associated benefits can be derived by completing a business risk assessment. This should help determine either direct savings or avoided costs from reduced overall risk levels as a result of the implemented security measures.

Let's shift to a business risk management focus. As a small business owner, you are concerned with risks that may jeopardize your business. Risks cover a wide variety of categories, which vary by industry sectors and are dependent on the types of products and services offered by an organization, and even by geographic location. For example, some of the risk categories include supply chain stability, ability to hire and retain skilled workers, regional and national economic conditions (e.g., recession), environmental conditions (e.g., "tornado alley" or earthquake zones), number and size of competing companies, ease of or barriers to entry into a particular market, and distribution channels. None of these examples are considered a cyber risk; however, all of them can impact computer systems. A cyberattack on business computer systems can also impact several of them. Chapters 3 and 4 will address cyber risk management in more detail.

Security, Compliance, and Risk Management

We will be looking at this topic from three perspectives. The first is security against cyberattacks. The second is a legal requirement for businesses to protect their data and their customers' data, as mandated by regulations for different industry sectors. The third perspective is looking at cybersecurity for emergency management planning.

Regulatory compliance is an important factor that drives a business to implement cybersecurity measures and may very well be why you picked up this book. One example of industry-wide security requirements is the Payment Card Industry Data Security Standards (PCI-DSS). These security standards apply to any business that processes debit or credit card payments from customers. However, meeting the security requirements for compliance does not mean that the resulting level of security is adequate for managing cyber risks at an acceptable level for the business. In other words, having "compliant" security may help you avoid being fined by the regulator for a security breach. However, it may not provide sufficient security to properly protect your sensitive data and prevent the breach in the first place.

Another area where an outside entity might require certain levels of security is the realm of cybersecurity insurance. Most insurance companies that provide this coverage have strict requirements for having appropriate types and levels of cybersecurity measures in place, including policies, procedures, and training. Insurance carrier requirements fall into the category of compliance, although not regulatory. The insurance premiums a company is charged assumes a basic level of cybersecurity maturity, and those premiums may decrease when additional levels of security are implemented. Having an overall cybersecurity program will go a long way toward addressing many insurance requirements. This includes written policies and procedures, an incident response plan, and an employee awareness and training program, all of which must be maintained and updated regularly (often annually).

Emergency management planning includes both disaster recovery (DR) and business continuity (BC). The business continuity plan (BCP) is intended to direct core business operations during an emergency incident. The disaster recovery plan (DRP) is intended to direct how the business can re-start basic operations after an emergency incident has ended, and contains the steps to restore normal business operations, if possible. Planning for the cybersecurity aspects of natural or man-made disasters should be included with general business planning for emergencies. You will need to ensure that security measures are functional, even if the business is operating at a baseline level. You will also need to ensure that backup data is secure since it will likely be used to restore your systems.

Protecting your business assets is common sense, whether from theft, fire, flood, vandalism, or cyberattack, but it doesn't have to be difficult or overly technical. Another consideration, in today's world of "cloud computing," is that many business applications are hosted on the Internet. A company's data may be stored on servers across multiple locations. This is different than in the past when a company owned its own servers. The servers were located in the same building as the company's main office, and they were managed by someone in the company or contracted by the company. One result of this shift in the computing environment is less focus on physical assets and more on digital assets. As discussed in an upcoming chapter, critical business assets, including information assets, need to be identified and categorized by risk level. Many businesses may still have quite a few physical assets to inventory. However, any business using cloud services should also concentrate on identifying their critical data and protecting it.

This may be a good place to go into a little more detail about cloud computing. This includes how your information is managed, stored, and transmitted by a CSP. You might have a very good contract for services, including what security the CSP is providing and an established incident response plan. That is all well and good; you need those assurances; however, you should also have a few security measures of your own. After all, your office computers (and maybe some portable laptops) will be accessing your data to conduct your business. One key point to keep in mind is that any confidential or sensitive information should be encrypted "at rest" and "in transit." This means when data is stored somewhere or when it is being transferred from one place to another across a network. There are plenty of inexpensive solutions, as well as some rather costly ones, that you can implement. Another key point is that all of your office computers should have an adequate level of security to protect against at least the most common types of cyberattacks. This will reduce the chance that an attacker can gain unauthorized access to your data hosted on a cloud service.

Basic Terminology – Defined

Before getting into more detail, now is a good time to mention some terminology used in general practice and throughout this book. Please refer to Appendix A for a detailed glossary of terms to help you understand some of the technical matters discussed later. For now, consider the terms "cybersecurity" and "information security" as being synonymous. The topic of this book could just as easily have been, "Creating an Information Security Program."

When you see "credentials" or "login credentials," it refers to the username (or ID) and a password or other secure method of logging in to a computer system. This is what most cybercriminals want to steal, so they can log in to your systems as you and perpetrate whatever criminal activity they want. These cybercriminals are seeking to find a hole in the security of your confidential or sensitive information. This would create a risk to what is known as the triad of cybersecurity – "C.I.A." – which stands for:

- Confidentiality of sensitive information (protecting against unauthorized access)
- Integrity of your data (protecting against destruction or alteration)
- Availability of your systems (protecting against disruption of services)

Another set of related terms we need to define upfront are threats, vulnerabilities, and risk. A "threat" is an event or circumstance with the potential to adversely impact an individual or organization, such as by causing financial loss, harm to its image or reputation, or disruption of its operations. A related term, "threat actor," is an individual or group of individuals who can carry out a threat. A "vulnerability" is a weakness in a system or software, a lack of proper security controls, or poorly configured security devices, which would allow for a system or software to be attacked. "Risk" (specifically, "cyber risk") is defined as the likelihood a particular threat will exploit a certain vulnerability.

From the field of risk management, we draw on the concept of controls or control measures, which includes the following:

- "Administrative Controls" are policies and other methods of controlling human behavior;

- "Operational Controls" include procedures and processes, either manual or automated, to perform certain tasks in a specified manner or sequence;
- "Technical Controls" are the computer and network security devices or software that is programmed or configured to perform automated security tasks. These also include configuration settings that allow or deny certain actions or behaviors; and
- "Countermeasures" are technical security controls specifically intended to defend against a particular attack vector or attack methodology.

All of these terms are meaningless if there is no target for an attack. The term "information asset" is used to describe an asset that is a potential target. It has value to the business, and any harm or loss to that asset could damage the business. You should also realize that some devices or equipment with a low business value may actually have value to some cybercriminals, for reasons beyond your business. Information assets are generally digital data (aka information) and the computer systems used for storing or processing the data. However, in some cases, other business assets, such as merchandise inventory, manufacturing equipment, vehicles, buildings, and people, may be considered by some to be information assets. To properly implement a cybersecurity program, you will need to have an accurate inventory of all information assets. Each one must be categorized by type of asset and classified by asset value. Then, assign a risk value based on a risk assessment. These assets may or may not include facilities, industrial control systems, plant automation systems, and other non-traditional computing systems (sometimes referred to as "Internet of Things" (IoT) devices or operational technology (OT)). Assigning values to these assets will be discussed in an upcoming chapter.

Chapter 1 – Key Points and Recommended Action Items

The following is a quick summary of the key points from this chapter:

- Almost all businesses will become the victim of a cyberattack; you should consider it a matter of **when** it will occur, not **if** it will.
- Small businesses that are not prepared for a cyberattack are more likely to go out of business due to the impacts of a cyberattack, should one occur.
- Don't regard cybersecurity as simply a business expense; you need to factor in the benefits of reducing overall business risk.
- Three perspectives for looking at cybersecurity include security (protecting your assets), compliance (meeting regulatory requirements), and emergency management (planning ahead for resilience), all of which enhance business risk management.
- If you are using cloud computing services for regular operations, ensure your confidential and sensitive information is protected with encryption.
- Learn and understand some of the basic terminology related to cybersecurity, so you can be conversant with vendors and service providers.

Here are some recommended actions you can take to start the process of developing a cybersecurity program for your small business:

- To get an overall picture of what's at stake, create a list of all the ways your business uses technology, both internally for staff and externally with customers and others (e.g., third-party business partners).
- Review your business plan and risk management plan and start to think about how cybersecurity measures can enable safe operations and reduce business risk.

- If you operate in a regulated industry, or if you process credit and debit card transactions, find out what regulatory or contractual requirements apply for cybersecurity.
- Review the security measures you already have in place, either through internal staff and procedures or through third-party contracts.

Refer to Appendix B for some resources to conduct further research into cybercrimes related specifically to your industry sector and to better understand the potential for becoming a victim.

Chapter 2

What You Need to Succeed

This book will provide you with all the information you need to create and implement a cybersecurity program for your small business. However, this book was not written in a vacuum. It draws on references and resources from several places that contribute to the success of small businesses. This book is intended as a starting point for those small businesses seeking to incorporate cybersecurity into their company culture and integrate cybersecurity governance into overall business governance. The resources contained in Appendix B are there to help with this process.

What Is Included in a Cybersecurity Program?

As a preview of the guidance provided throughout the rest of the book, Figure 2-1 below contains a short outline of the business documents frequently used to create and implement a cybersecurity program in a small/medium business (SMB). You will most likely only need a few of these documents, and this book will help you choose the specific components and content to customize the program to your individual needs. You will find examples and templates for the governance documents in Appendix D.

Business Governance Document
- Business Plan (with Risk Management including cyber risks)

Cybersecurity Governance Documents
- Cybersecurity Strategy
- Cybersecurity Program Definition
- Cybersecurity Policies & Procedures*
- Cybersecurity Awareness & Training Program
- Cybersecurity Incident Response Plan

Figure 2-1. Outline of Recommended Governance Documents

*The recommended minimum set of cybersecurity policies and procedures for SMBs to implement include:

- User account management (identity and access management)
- Internet and email acceptable use
- Protecting sensitive and confidential information
- Use of virtual private networks (VPN) and encryption
- Remote access
- Software updates and patch management
- Portable or mobile device security
- System administration security
- Third-party access
- Identity theft awareness and training (FTC Red Flag Rule)

Most of these policies can be combined as short sections within an overall cybersecurity policy, which is the way the template in Appendix D is written. Some of these policies may not apply to your particular business and may not be necessary, as explained later.

What is Behind Door Number Three?

You might be wondering where the idea of writing this book came from, and what the basis is for the content of each chapter and the related recommendations. Over ten years of consulting with and offering free training to small businesses, coupled with the trend that small businesses are increasingly becoming targets of cybercrimes, made the need for this book apparent. We have based the content of this book and its recommendations on well-known national and international standards, business best practices that have been used and recommended by other experts for many years, and over twenty years of personal experience. We are attempting to bring together in one place all the information you need for your small business to be successful in cybersecurity. Below, we offer a summary of the major sources used in the creation of this book and the guidance included in upcoming chapters.

First, information related to general business structure and planning came from the Small Business Administration (SBA) and their technical partner, SCORE. This includes the outline for a business plan and the summary of the components of a risk management plan. There is a hierarchy of business documents in Chapter 5 that combines practices for business governance from the SBA and a compilation of IT and cybersecurity governance practices observed in public sector and private sector organizations. Second, the information presented throughout this book came from sources whose recommendations have been used successfully in medium-sized and large organizations; now we are scaling them down for small businesses.

Another resource that has been supporting cybersecurity and IT professionals for over 30 years is the SANS Institute. This was also the birthplace for the Top 20 Critical Security Controls, which are now the CIS Controls®. SANS conducts research and provides training in several topic areas as well as at different levels, from basic fundamentals up to advanced concepts and skills. This book is indebted to the wide range of professionals who contributed to the best practices and materials produced by SANS, which have influenced the author over many years.

The use of industry standards, where possible, has been recommended across industry sectors for businesses of all sizes by management consultants and regulatory agencies for several decades. If an industry has a set of standards, it makes it easier to compare one business against another within the same industry sector. In regulated industries, it is easier for the regulatory agency to judge whether or not a business is meeting the regulatory compliance standards. In the realm of the U.S. federal government and all of its agencies, departments, bureaus, and contracted private companies, the standards for cybersecurity fall under the National Institute of Standards and Technology (NIST), which is part of the Department of Commerce. Even businesses that do not fall under mandatory compliance with NIST standards can still benefit from them. However, trying to figure out which of the hundreds of standards you should implement as a small business is a formidable task. This brings us to our next set of standards – the CIS Controls®.

What started out as the SANS Top 20 Critical Security Controls became a vetted set of basic control measures that almost any organization could implement, even as a starting point toward achieving the NIST standards. SANS managed the controls for versions 1 through 4; for version 5, they were managed by the Council on Cyber Security (Le Counseil de la Cyber Sécurité), a global non-profit dedicated to security for an open Internet, and had the title, "The Critical Security Controls for Effective Cyber Defense."

The Center for Internet Security (CIS) took over for version 6 of the controls, released in October 2015. Since then, version 6.1 was released in August 2016, version 7 was released in March 2018, and most recently, version 7.1 was released in April 2019. Along with version 7.1, CIS created three Implementation Groups, which consist of various Sub-Controls that should be implemented based on the characteristics of the organizations that fit into each group. These group characteristics start with the size of an organization and then focus on (1) data sensitivity and criticality of services offered, (2) level of technical expertise of staff within the organization or under contract, and (3) resources available and dedicated toward cybersecurity. Most small businesses will fall within the first Implementation Group, which is the focus of this book.

To help businesses implement the CIS Controls, CIS also publishes several companion guides on specific topics, which provide details beyond what is contained in the basic controls. In addition, CIS publishes a metrics and measurements document to help organizations validate the effectiveness of the controls they are using. Finally, there is the CIS risk assessment method (CIS RAM), which provides templates and instructions to help organizations conduct risk assessments. This tool is not dependent on the CIS Controls and can be used in almost any business environment. You will learn more about risk management in Section 2.

Next, we will start by using a risk management perspective in viewing cybersecurity in relation to other business risks.

Section 2

Cybersecurity as Risk Management

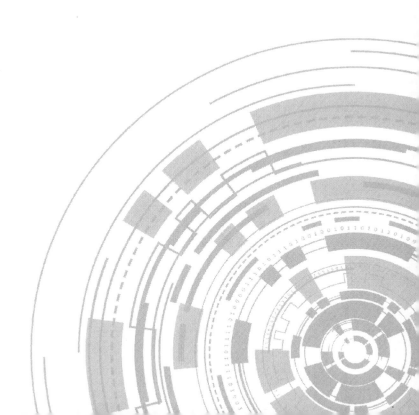

One of the great challenges we face in business is balancing risk and reward. Without sufficient risk, there is rarely sufficient reward to justify the energy spent in any endeavor. But if we take on too much risk, we often regret it far more than we celebrate our successes. It can lead to business failure. So, we seek ways to manage, or mitigate, our risks. We avoid certain activities, we buy insurance, we implement safety procedures, we monitor, and we report. So that we know which activities are riskier than others and therefore how to apply our mitigation, we've developed risk measurement techniques and we've applied them throughout most of our business domains. In this section, we're going to explore how you can make a cybersecurity risk management perspective work for you.

Chapter 3

Applying a Cybersecurity Risk Perspective to Your Business

When creating a new business, and periodically over the life of a business, we usually work with a business plan that defines the overall purpose, goals, and objectives, and often includes a business risk management plan. As we discuss in this chapter and the following chapter, planning ahead and incorporating cybersecurity concepts into the business plan and risk management plan will benefit business operations by taking into account and mitigating cyber risk factors, in the same manner as addressing other business risks.

The risk management plan should describe the business' risk tolerance posture – somewhere on a continuum from risk-averse to risk-tolerant. To be "risk-averse" means the organization wants as little risk as possible; while "none" would be great, it is unrealistic, as all businesses have some risks. The business attitude is generally to take all reasonable steps to minimize risks. To be "risk-tolerant" does not mean the organization wants to have high levels of risk; rather, it means a willingness to accept certain levels of risk for particular assets or under certain circumstances. In general, this means the costs to mitigate or eliminate such risks exceed the business value of an asset or the damage/harm that would occur to the business if the asset were compromised. Even risk-averse businesses will have defined levels of acceptable risk.

During the early stages of the business planning process, many companies perform a SWOT analysis to assess the company's abilities and the condition of the intended business environment. SWOT stands for Strengths, Weaknesses, Opportunities, and

Threats, and the output is useful in several sections of the business plan. The first two factors are conditions that are internal to the organization, while the second two factors are controlled by external forces. However, there is a definite cross-over between all four factors – internal strengths or weaknesses can impact the company's ability to take advantage of market opportunities or to defend against threats in the business environment. While these factors are applied to general business operations, they can also be used to analyze cybersecurity-related aspects of the business.

Identifying Cyber Aspects of a Business Plan

Let's look at the primary sections commonly used in a business plan derived from a Small Business Administration (SBA) template (refer to Appendix C) and discover how and where technology enables the business and cybersecurity threats add risk. For convenience, we provide a summary table near the end of the chapter. First, the business plan usually starts with a mission statement (sometimes referred to as a purpose statement), which defines the overarching mission or purpose for the business. It answers two basic questions: "Why does this business exist?" and "What does this business do?" The mission statement generally does not include operational details, although it might mention a certain business approach or methodology which, in turn, could point to the use of technology. Here are two examples of mission statements: (1) "XYZ Company is a privately-owned business, and our mission is to provide our customers with the most reliable and fastest courier and delivery service in the region while protecting the confidentiality of our customers' package contents." (2) "The mission of ABC Corporation is to produce the highest-quality electronic components for use in ultra-high-resolution digital monitors." Applying a cybersecurity risk perspective really starts with the second section of our example business plan – the business goals and objectives.

Almost every business today uses technology to achieve its goals and objectives. It may start by simply using email, having a basic finance or accounting program, and keeping a customer list. It may also include more complex systems that manage a supply chain, production, and distribution channels. While many small businesses do not have a dedicated website, most have at least an informational web page that lists their products or services, hours of operation, and contact information. All of these uses of technology have an accompanying cyber risk, which could impact the business's ability to achieve its goals and objectives. We will discuss those risks after reviewing other sections of the business plan. While we are discussing the sections of the business plan and identifying related cyber risks, it should be noted that the actual cyber risk information is not generally included in the business plan. The general cyber risk information should be part of an overall risk management plan, and the cybersecurity details should be part of the cybersecurity program description.

Next, let's look at a series of questions related to your business operations. Answering these questions will help you determine some of the technologies you will use in your small business. Knowing with whom and how you interact to conduct business can also help you identify security requirements and assist with a potential threat model analysis (if one is conducted). Some basic, overall questions include:

- Who are your customers or clients (are they local, regional, or global)?
- How will they interact with you to conduct business (e.g., online website, telephone, in-person at an office or storefront, or a combination of methods)?
- What customer information (e.g., personal data, personally identifiable information, etc.) will you collect and save for future reference? (Refer to Chapter 7 on privacy.)
- If applicable, who are your suppliers and service providers, and how will you conduct business with them?

- Are there any other businesses with which you partner to provide services or products, and how is that business relationship managed?

Now, we will add some questions related to technology, drilling down to the next layer of how you plan to use technology and starting to identify what technologies might be used:

- Does your small business have its own website?
- Is the website just informational? Is it used for eCommerce, or is it also used to transact business with other companies in your supply and distribution chain (B2B)?
- Who maintains the data and content on the website?
- Who is responsible for the security on the website, especially for financial transactions, but also for protecting any confidential data, such as your customers' private information?
- Besides the website, what other systems are used by employees, and what systems are shared with customers, suppliers, distributors, and other business partners?
- Who is responsible for managing those systems?

There are many other questions you may want to ask and address, eventually, but these are a good start.

For your business' products and services – the core of your business – think about how much you depend on technology. Be aware that this aspect of cyber risk analysis is probably the most complex of the business plan components, so don't get discouraged; just break it down into workable sub-components. If your business deals with products, virtually every aspect can have a technology component – research and development, the supply chain, manufacturing, distribution. For service-related businesses, your "product" consists of human skills and abilities to perform the services you offer. Depending on the nature of your services, your requirements may include suppliers, research and development, referral resources, use of disposable or consumable supplies, and fleet vehicles. You might also create or offer new services over time, which could be the result of market research on customer needs and developing the skills and abilities to perform a new service.

Product-oriented businesses may have automated connections with suppliers through materials inventory using automated low stock re-order points. Even without automatic supply ordering, you likely have online accounts with each supplier, and they may have accounts on your systems. Then, you have all of the sales transactions, which includes processing of returned items, so you need secure customer payment methods, as well as security measures to protect against refund fraud. At the other end of the process, it's also likely you have online accounts with your distributors or shipping companies, and, in some cases, they might have accounts on your systems.

From an internal business perspective, you should have a marketing plan for getting your products or services to your target customers. Conducting general market analysis and more specific competitor analysis will involve the use of technology. Searching the Internet is a common method of gathering information, while malicious websites that mimic legitimate sites are one of the primary attack vectors. However, before we get ahead of ourselves let's finish discussing a few more sections of the business plan. Another critical area where technology is needed is for your business' financial accounting. This can be done using a simple spreadsheet on your local computer or laptop, or it can be a hosted application from a third-party service provider.

The next aspect of a business plan addresses operational planning, which may include, for example, where the business office will be located and whether or not there will be other field offices. Additional examples include the type of work that will be performed at each location, and what type of positions and how many staff there are at each location. This section is where the legal and legislative or regulatory environment for your industry sector is described, which, in the United States, should cover local/regional, state, and federal laws and regulations, as applicable. If your business conducts transactions with customers in other countries, you must also address the legal requirements of those jurisdictions, especially with regards to the customer information, such as the European GDPR (General Data Protection Regulation). Finally, in this section of the business plan, you should describe the business policies related to billing and payments.

The final sections of the business plan address different aspects of finance, from startup expenses and investors providing startup capital, to creating and managing an annual budget. Financial planning is a critical function for any business, including having accurate forecasts of income and expenses, properly tracking ongoing transactions, and validating daily account activity and balances.

Applying a Cybersecurity Perspective to Your Business Plan

Now that we have basic descriptions for the main sections of the business plan, we're ready to incorporate the cybersecurity perspective. Remember, one underlying purpose of cyber-attacks is to impact the confidentiality, integrity, and availability of your business data, and there are many methods and attack vectors used. Examples of common attack vectors include (1) a "phishing" email containing a link to a false website that captures your login credentials, (2) a malicious website which mimics a legitimate site and hosts malware (such as computer viruses, worms, or Trojan horse software), or (3) a standard email message with a file attachment that contains malware.

Your business goals and objectives may be to produce a minimum number of widgets per year, or to have the highest customer satisfaction rating in your industry sector among regional competitors, or to achieve a minimum level of monthly revenue. In evaluating the risk levels and impacts on the business, if you are not able to achieve a certain goal or objective, a cyber risk may have the same impact as a natural disaster (flood, earthquake, fire, or tornado), because the resulting impact to the business is the same.

One example of a technology that supports the tracking of business goals and objectives is workflow software that schedules components for each stage of a manufacturing process and monitors how long it takes at each step. Another example is a customer relationship management (CRM) package that performs many functions, one of which is keeping track of incoming customer phone calls, how quickly they are answered, average time on hold, and the average length of a call. It may also be used to track customer satisfaction. Assuming there are business goals related to the efficiency of manufacturing processes and customer service, then these systems need security measures to ensure they function as planned. Protecting those systems and technologies will probably lower the risk levels across the business because those systems support more than just achieving your goals and objectives – they probably service the core of your business.

Potential cyber threats that may impact these systems include direct hacking attempts to infiltrate the systems, steal or damage critical business information, or launch ransomware, which encrypts all of your files and prevents access to your own data. Another common type of attack is a denial of service (DoS), where your computers are overwhelmed with millions of false data requests so that they can't perform their normal functions.

This brings us to your primary business operations, including customer/client interaction and your products and/or services. There are two primary categories of information or data that fall into this area – (1) external data related to people or organizations outside of your company, and (2) internal data you create and maintain related to your business functions. While cyber threats and security measures may be similar for both categories, we will address them separately, to give you a better understanding of the technology systems used for each purpose.

How you use technology to interact with customers, suppliers, distributors, and other third parties is a critical factor to consider for risk management. For the purpose of simplifying this discussion, we will use the term "third party" to refer to anyone outside of your business. You will need to take into account which of your systems are used for direct third-party contact, such as a website where customers can place orders and make payments. You also need to consider any system that might store third-party information, and where that information might be transferred between the initial system and any others. Earlier in this chapter, there was a series of questions on this topic, and now you need to identify areas of potential cyber risks that could damage or destroy your business. This is one area where you might consider hiring a cybersecurity professional to perform an initial assessment and set up some basic security measures.

In addition to the need for general cybersecurity measures, you will also need to address privacy regulations – General Data Protection Regulation (GDPR) in Europe and the California Consumer Privacy Act (CCPA) are examples of such privacy regulations. These regulations dictate how you handle customers' personal information and require a privacy program for your business.

You should protect your own intellectual property rights, including any proprietary and confidential information about your products and services. You may not have any trade secrets, per se, but you probably have information or a business process that can give you a competitive advantage. That type of information is worth protecting. You will need to identify all systems containing that information and to where it might be transferred, especially when using cloud services.

The cyber risks related to this area of business operations include the potential direct attacks against your web server or other applications running on the same server, and attacks against your internal servers (if any), workstations, and laptops. These types of attacks are happening every day to businesses around the world. The two most common types of attacks are from ransomware and denial of service. Ransomware has been in the news quite a lot and gets its name from the fact that it encrypts all the files on a system, and then you get a ransom demand to pay for the key to unlock your files. Most commonly, your computers can become infected with ransomware from clicking a link in a phishing email message or through a malicious website, where your browser was directed without you knowing it. The denial of service (DoS) attack consists of one or more (often thousands) attack computers sending thousands or millions of bogus data requests to your server. This attack overwhelms your server resources to the extent that normal transactions cannot occur, even though the server is still running, as opposed to a different type of attack that would "crash" the server.

Being a specific target of an attack depends on several factors, including the following:

- being in an industry that is targeted more than others
- being in a geographic location where attacks are higher than average
- being part of a well-known brand or receiving public recognition which draws the attention of attackers
- having vulnerable systems on the Internet which can be scanned and easily located

Taking into account these underlying factors and associated cyber risks will ultimately lower the overall business risk level. You should be able to eliminate or at least mitigate several risk factors, resulting in reduced risk of cyberattacks. The first three factors above are all external to your small business and largely out of your control. However, practicing general cyber hygiene to keep your systems safe will lower your risk of attack. The last factor above would become known as a result of conducting a vulnerability assessment. In this case, you should take the recommended actions to mitigate each specific vulnerability.

Lastly, we reach the area of finance and accounting for your business plan. As you might imagine, for cybercriminals, it's all about the money. Keeping your financial records and transactions secure might be the most critical requirement for having appropriate security measures in place. Your business plan probably doesn't specify the type of accounting system you want to use; however, it would be good to specify how your accounting is going to be managed. There are three basic options to consider, each with somewhat different security requirements:

- You can manage finances internally within your small business, using internal computer systems and stand-alone accounting software.
- You can manage finances internally using your small business staff and a cloud-based accounting system.
- You can outsource the management of your small business finances to an outside accounting company.

For the first two options, you will be responsible for ensuring there are adequate and proper security measures in place, while the third option places that responsibility on the accounting firm. You will still need to have security measures in place between your computer systems and the accounting firm's systems, which includes procedures and safeguards against fraudulent transactions. One common and successful type of attack against financial and accounting services is called business email compromise (BEC), where office staff is tricked into executing a transfer of funds based on an email that appears to come from their management, without proper verification or validation of the message. Several different procedures can be implemented to avoid this type of fraud, such as never allowing email to be used for authorizing fund transfers. Other cyberattacks related to money are direct attacks against either the accounting database or trying to capture the data being transferred across the network between the business' accounting system and the bank.

In general, the business plan should take into account any time you are using outside (third-party) services, either directly from a supplier or another company, or from a cloud service provider. The terms and conditions of the contracts for those business relationships must have language that fully covers the areas of responsibility and liability for protecting your small business information assets.

To summarize the business plan components and their potential cyber risks, the following checklist covers the basic topics and the related technology or security issues that may or may not apply to your particular business.

Chapter 4

A Cybersecurity Risk Assessment Methodology

There is a plethora of information covering different aspects of risk management and how to conduct risk assessments. An Internet search will provide dozens of professional consulting firms offering to perform risk assessments, each using their own methodology. You will find that risk assessment terms abound, such as "Single Loss Expectancy" (SLE), "Annualized Rate of Occurrence" (ARO), and "Annual Loss Expectancy" (ALE), which is the result of SLE multiplied by ARO.

One point of general agreement among all the methods is that the cost or burden of corrective control measures should never be more than the cost impact of the risk itself. In other words, you would never use a $1,000 solution for a $100 problem. There is also general agreement about the two primary types of risk assessments (below) and, for a complete risk picture of your small business, both types of assessments are needed:

- Quantitative (usually assigning numeric values)
- Qualitative (usually a ranking, such as high, medium, and low).

Small Business Focus – A Shortcut Assessment to Get Started

Before you can start an assessment, you have to understand what is being assessed. In other words, determine which assets, people, processes, or other operations will be part of the assessment. Regardless of which methodology is selected, a business needs to identify the assets that are critical for its operations. This includes information assets and other operational assets which support the core functions of the business, so you can prioritize what will be assessed. Examples of information assets could be the company's interactive web site where customers conduct business transactions, the database of customer information with payment card data, or a server where proprietary trade secrets are stored. Examples of operational assets could be physical equipment used in manufacturing your primary product, fleet vehicles used to deliver products or provide services to your customers, or specialized equipment used to provide services (which might be a laptop or tablet with custom applications).

The rest of this chapter and Appendix C go into detail about conducting a simple risk assessment. This can be difficult and time-consuming, so let's look instead at an alternative approach to help you save time and prioritize your high-value critical assets. First, read through the next section, which discusses an example risk matrix. Second, read through the rest of the chapter to get an understanding of what is involved in a basic risk assessment using a standard methodology.

To simplify the process of determining a risk level for your information assets, you only need to consider the "Level of Impact" and not the "Likelihood of Occurrence." The key part of estimating the impact on the business for the loss of a particular asset is assigning a business value to each asset. Once that value is determined, you can prioritize your critical assets from highest to lowest in risk value. The following section describes some tangible and intangible cost factors that help establish a business value. Here are some examples of potential assets you might have:

- Web applications that process customer transactions (e.g., sales, payments, etc.)
- Customer databases that contain confidential client information

- Servers or workstations that contain proprietary information (e.g., R&D or trade secrets) or other types of data that provide you with a competitive advantage
- Business systems that provide daily operational functions for your business
- Monitoring systems that check for compliance with regulatory requirements
- Accounting systems that contain your financial records
- Payroll or human resources systems that contain confidential employee information

You may find that there are some other steps you are able to take to enhance the business value of your assets. Once you have completed this process, you should use your prioritized list of assets to allocate security funding to protect the highest value assets, which if compromised would result in the greatest impact to the business.

Example Risk Assessment Matrix

You may already use a business risk assessment methodology. The main point of this chapter is to recommend a standardized risk assessment methodology. If you prefer not to use the one discussed here, choose one that fits your needs and stick with it. Using a standard methodology over time provides consistency in the manner that assessments are conducted and provides direct comparisons with prior assessments. A standardized methodology will provide a series of steps to follow. It usually starts with planning and preparation, then conducting the assessment, and performing necessary analyses. It concludes with summarizing the results and identifying actions to be taken to lower overall risk. While the process needs to address the specific critical assets, you do not need to conduct an assessment on each individual asset. Rather, you would assess similar classes of assets in a group and make any adjustments in the final risk rating for the individual assets in the group.

The organization's risk management plan should include a strategy for how the business is going to define and categorize risks, and the levels of acceptable risk for different business assets. It should further describe how to perform periodic risk assessments and how to mitigate and respond to different types of risk. Cybersecurity risk should simply be incorporated as a category of business risk. Calculating risk levels for cyber threats can generally use the same formulas as those for other types of business risk. One basic method, among many possibilities, is to assign values (usually on a scale of 1 to 5 or 1 to 10) for two risk parameters. The first is for the likelihood of a threat actually occurring as an attack against the organization. The second is for the level of impact on the business, which can be operational or financial. This is depicted in Figure 3-1 below. However, before you can assign a rating for the business impact, you must first evaluate each information asset and determine its business value. This will be addressed later.

In the following chart, the vertical axis, "Level of Impact," represents the severity of consequences to the business, based on the asset's determined business value. Remember, this asset value covers the cost of losing access to the data or the unauthorized release of confidential or proprietary information. The value includes things like tangible costs to recover and restore data, regulatory fines, breach notification, and identity theft protection. In addition, there are intangible costs, such as negative publicity, which undermines company integrity and brand name recognition. Along the horizontal axis, "Likelihood of Occurrence" represents the results of a vulnerability assessment and threat analysis for each asset. This results in a calculated possibility that a known threat will result in the exploitation of a vulnerability related to a target asset. The value assigned to an asset for this risk element is influenced by several internal and external factors, including:

- whether or not the asset actually has certain vulnerabilities and whether they are mitigated

- whether or not there is a known exploit for a particular vulnerability that was found
- cybersecurity and other security measures in place (e.g., facility security)
- industry trends for cyberattacks against similar organizations with similar computer systems
- threat intelligence reports regarding specific threat actors who may want to target the asset or a particular business

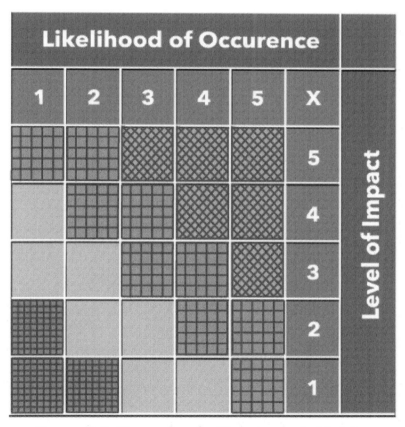

Figure 4-1. **Example of a Risk Analysis Matrix**

This example risk matrix has been divided into four risk categories, as indicated by the different hashes. The hashes correlate to a risk level, where lower-left hash indicates low risk, next hash indicates medium-low risk, next indicates medium-high risk, and upper-right indicates high risk. This style is sometimes called a "heat map" because when rendered in color, the areas in the upper half of the diagonal are orange and red, considered "hot" targets with high risk. The boxes included in each category are determined by the risk tolerance of the organization. It may shift to the lower-left for more risk-averse companies, meaning there are more medium-high and high boxes risk boxes in the upper-right diagonal and fewer low and medium boxes in the lower-left diagonal. Or, it may shift to the upper-right for more risk-tolerant companies, with fewer medium-high and high boxes and more of the low and medium boxes.

Introduction to the CIS Risk Assessment Method

Later in the book, when going through the steps of creating your cybersecurity program, we recommend the use of the CIS Controls as a standard set of security measures. In conjunction with those controls, the Center for Internet Security also provides a related Risk Assessment Method (CIS RAM).[3] While the CIS Risk Assessment Method is correlated with the CIS Controls, the methodology can be used on its own, in almost any circumstance. It is a vendor-neutral tool that is applicable across any industry sector. One key factor of the CIS Risk Assessment Method is evaluating the corrective measures using the same criteria as the risks, so they can be easily compared. Because the CIS Risk Assessment Method is provided openly to the cybersecurity community, we will use it as our example methodology. We will focus on *Risk Capability Tier 1*, based on the NIST (National Institute of Standards and Technology) Risk Management Framework (Special Publication 800-37, Rev. 2, issued in December 2018). If you have a more complex environment, you

---

[3] This work is licensed under a Creative Commons Attribution-Non Commercial-No Derivatives 4.0 International Public License
https://creativecommons.org/licenses/by-nc-nd/4.0/legalcode

could use the methodology in the NIST framework as an alternative to the CIS Risk Assessment Method. Related documents include NIST Special Publication 800-30, Revision 1, "Guide for Conducting Risk Assessments," issued in September 2012, and Special Publication 800-39, "Managing Information Security Risk," issued in March 2011.

The CIS Risk Assessment Method provides a framework with detailed instructions on how to conduct a thorough risk assessment as a project. It is set up this way because it is more likely to be successful and produce measurable results if it is set up and managed as a project. This includes defined roles and responsibilities, a specific scope, and a timeline. Even for your small business, following the simple steps in the framework will help ensure that you don't miss something important. The assessments can be done by a team (3 to 5 employees) or by just the small business owner. The sample project plan provided with the CIS Risk Assessment Method includes just five primary tasks and a few sub-tasks:

1. Defining the Scope and Scheduling Sessions
2. Defining the Risk Assessment Criteria
3. Defining the Risk Acceptance Criteria
4. Risk Assessment (Control-Based)
    4.1 Gather Evidence
    4.2 Model the Threats
    4.3 Risk Evaluation
5. Propose Safeguards
    5.1 Evaluate the Safeguards

The scope should specifically identify the critical assets which will be part of the assessment, including both physical assets and information assets. If possible, you should identify the owner of each asset, which should be a role/position within the organization (such as the COO, CFO, or CIO). Also, identify the custodian of the asset, which is the role/position responsible for daily operation and maintenance (such as the IT group). The asset owner should be providing key information related to the asset value and its business impact. The asset custodian should provide information related to threats and vulnerabilities.

Conducting a Risk Assessment

When conducting a risk assessment, there are three principles to keep in mind, which follow the Duty of Care Risk Analysis (DoCRA) doctrine. These principles are often used by insurance companies in evaluating breach claims. The phases and steps within the CIS Risk Assessment Method framework are intended to provide minimum standards of care in conducting risk assessments. Following these standards should help you show that you have performed your due diligence, and you are basing your risk analysis on recognized standards (in case of an audit or a data breach). The three principles are:

1. Risk analysis must consider the interests of all parties that may be harmed by the risk.
2. Risks must be reduced to a level that authorities and potentially affected parties would find appropriate.
3. Safeguards must not be more burdensome than the risks they protect against.

The actual risk assessment involves evaluating the risk factors and impact criteria for each identified critical asset. You'll need to add a text definition for each of the five rating criteria for the likelihood of occurrence and for the level of impact when you use the example risk matrix. The CIS Risk Assessment Method uses two criteria for the impact – one for the impact to the organization's mission, and one for the impact to the organization's obligations (to prevent harm to others). Using definition tables for each factor and a simple calculation table, the CIS Risk Assessment Method makes it easy to rate each asset.

Below is an example of the impact criteria using a five-point scale (refer to the Risk Assessment Method documentation for details). In each column, you are describing the potential impact of the threat.

Impact Level	Impact to Our Mission (List the effect on your organization's capabilities at the various impact levels)	Impact to Our Obligations (List the effect on your organization's customers or partners at the various impact levels)
1	Describe a scenario where the consequences would be acceptable by all parties (for example: you are able to conduct business and provide services or products to your customers)	Describe a scenario where the consequences would be acceptable to outside parties who could be harmed (for example: your customers' and partners' confidential information is adequately protected)
2	Describe a scenario where the consequences would be mostly acceptable by all parties, and would be recoverable (for example: a few business processes are impacted, resulting in delays for some products or services; a few products have flaws, but still within planned variances)	Describe a scenario where the consequences would be mostly acceptable to outside parties who could be harmed, and would be recoverable (for example: some customer or partner information has been accessed by unauthorized persons; however, none of it was confidential information)
3	Describe a scenario where the consequences would be mostly unacceptable by all parties, but would be recoverable (for example: several business processes are impacted, causing long delays in providing services or products to customers; some products have moderate flaws)	Describe a scenario where the consequences would be mostly unacceptable to others, but would be recoverable (for example: your customer or partner information was accessed by unauthorized persons, but the confidential information was encrypted)
4	Describe a scenario where the consequences would be unacceptable by all parties, and recovery would be difficult (for example: most business processes are impacted and very few products or services can be provided to customers; several products have significant flaws)	Describe a scenario where the consequences would be unacceptable to others, and recovery would be difficult (for example: one or more of your customers or partners became a victim of a cybercrime, resulting from unauthorized access of their confidential information stored on your systems)
5	Describe a scenario from which the organization could not recover (for example: all business functions are impacted and no products or services can be provided to customers)	Describe a scenario from which others could not recover (for example: your partners' proprietary and confidential information was taken from your business systems, resulting in their loss of business)

Table 4-1

In the column labeled "Impact to Our Mission" each of the effects would be to your capabilities – the threat degrades your capabilities to some extent. This starts with minimal impact at impact level 1 and increases to the maximum impact possible from that threat at level 5. In the column labeled "Impact to Our Obligations" each of the effects would be to your customers or partners. Again, minimal at level 1, increasing to the maximum possible impact at level 5.

A similar table is used to define and describe the Likelihood of Occurrence criteria:

Likelihood Score	Likelihood - Foreseeability
1	Not foreseeable; threat/risk is not likely in the current environment
2	Slightly foreseeable; threat/risk is plausible, but not likely; no known activity in the global environment
3	Somewhat foreseeable; possibility that threat/risk will occur, but not expected
4	Probably will occur; moderate likelihood that threat/risk will occur, based on evidence of similar activity in the global environment
5	Expected to occur; strong certainty that threat/risk will occur at some time

Table 4-2

Finally, the CIS Risk Assessment Method has a formula for calculating the risk value for each asset based on the scores assigned for each of the criteria above. This is called the "Observed Risk" score. You would then pick an "Acceptable Risk Level" and use the results of this exercise to prioritize the risks that you want to mitigate.

For example, you might decide that an acceptable risk level is 9 (impact level three, perhaps you'll call that "moderate" and likelihood 3, somewhat foreseeable). You might then prioritize mitigating risks with a score of 10 or greater that have a likelihood of 3 or greater.

Impact Score	X	Likelihood Score	=	Risk Value
{1 - 5}	X	{1 - 5}	=	{1 - 25}
... therefore ...				
Acceptable Risk			≤	{RV}

Figure 4-2

The same three steps are used to rate the proposed "Safeguards," which are the security controls, devices, and procedures used to protect the asset. The result of this evaluation and calculation is the "Safeguard Risk" score, which is compared against the Observed Risk for the same asset. At this point, you can determine whether additional security measures would be beneficial or not.

Some Final Steps in a Risk Assessment

The purpose here is not to replicate all of the CIS Risk Assessment Method steps and instructions, but to give you an overview of the larger process. Hopefully, you can understand and plan for what needs to be done. One additional step will be the creation of a "Risk Register" to identify the controls currently in place, known vulnerabilities, and known threats. This will help further define risk levels and likelihood of occurrence. The risk register leads to creating a threat model to cover a group of similar assets. The threat model is used to identify what additional controls are needed to fill any security gaps. The risk register is also where you would use the dual impact factor ("impact to company" vs. "impact to others"). Here you multiply the likelihood value by the higher of the two impact values. The CIS Risk Assessment Method documentation provides detailed instructions, along with examples and templates for all of these tasks.

The final steps in the process cover "Risk Treatment," or how the organization chooses to address each of the risks and safeguards. The proposed solutions to increase security and reduce risk must be both:

- *Appropriate* - remaining risks will not create or increase harm beyond what is tolerable
- *Reasonable* - safeguards will not cause more of a burden than the risks they are meant to protect against

One thing worth mentioning is that any proposed safeguard should not introduce new risks. In other words, be careful not to break existing processes or add a new process so complex as to introduce new failures where none existed before.

As a small business with a relatively small number of critical assets, you don't need to go into the detail of the risk register unless you want to. Just using the rating formula to find risk values for each asset, then finding the corresponding safeguard values, and comparing them, may be all that you need.

Chapter 4 – Key Points and Recommended Action Items

The following is a quick summary of the key points from this chapter:

- The field of risk management now incorporates the use of cyber risk assessments as part of an overall business risk analysis.

- A complete risk assessment includes both quantitative risks, resulting in a numeric risk value (which may include a dollar amount), and qualitative risks, resulting in a relative risk ranking (such as high, medium or low).

- Determine how the organization wants to address the identified risks for each asset, keeping in mind that the solution must be both appropriate and reasonable.

- You should select an appropriate, standardized risk assessment methodology that you will use over several years; this will provide consistency in analysis and comparisons. The CIS Risk Assessment Method (CIS RAM) is recommended because it correlates with the CIS Controls, which are used as the basis for the cybersecurity program.

- Organizations should use due care when conducting risk assessments and follow the procedures in the selected, standardized methodology.

- Use the applicable rating and ranking tools provided in the methodology; for example, computing the "Likelihood of Occurrence" and potential "Business Impact" for both the identified risk and the related corrective measures ("safeguards"). This provides a direct correlation between the risk and the countermeasures.

- Be prepared to conduct an overall risk assessment on an annual basis, or an ad hoc assessment whenever new critical assets are being placed into service.

Here are some simple actions you can take to select an appropriate cyber risk assessment methodology for your small business:

- Download and read the CIS Risk Assessment Method documentation to fully understand the methodology and how it can be applied to your small business. Plan to use this methodology for at least five years, to provide consistency. Document it along with the basic process in your governance documents, specifically in the risk management plan.

- If you already use a different risk assessment methodology or you elect to choose a different one, ensure that it is documented to include cyber risks and follow the other action items presented here.

- Start with just a few critical assets to conduct your first risk assessment with the new methodology. This will help you learn the necessary procedures and analyses without becoming overwhelmed. As you better understand the process, expand the risk assessment to include more assets until all of them have been assessed.

Defining your Cybersecurity Plan

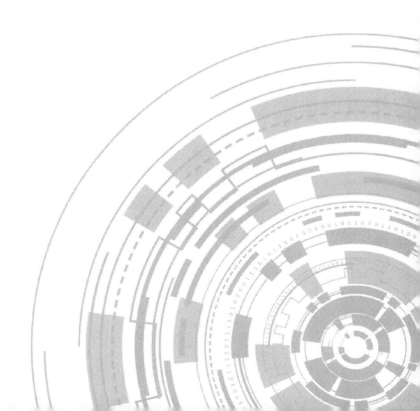

Section 3 is devoted to defining your cybersecurity plan. In Chapter 5 I'll help you define the elements of your plan. We'll discuss those elements in relation to your company's overall strategic and operational plans. This will help you present your cybersecurity strategy in a business context and make you a better business partner.

In Chapter 6 we go a step further and dive into the essential lifecycles that will allow you to operate your cybersecurity program as a series of repeatable processes. This process orientation, represented as lifecycles, provides the discipline you'll need to keep your processes growing and maturing in step with the business.

Then in Chapter 7 we will address the special privacy requirements imposed by the various jurisdictions and how they should inform your security program. As many cybersecurity professionals are fond of saying, you can't have privacy without security.

Chapter 5

Defining the Elements of a Small Business Cybersecurity Program

There are two basic categories of documents for a cybersecurity program. The first category includes business governance documents, and the second category includes documents defining technical components. The intent of this chapter is to make it easy for non-technical owners or managers to incorporate these documents into an existing business plan. This chapter focuses on the documents encompassing governance and related policies and procedures. Several technical processes that can be automated during implementation will be covered in Section 5. The specific components from each category will vary from business to business, just as there are differences between a small restaurant, a dry cleaner, and an automotive repair shop.

The following diagram (Figure 5-1) provides an example of a complete set of governance documents. It may not be necessary to have some of these documents for your small business; each business' requirements will differ. The diagram also illustrates how cybersecurity program documents fit into the business structure. In the subsequent document descriptions, the term "high-level business documents" refers to those overarching documents which define the business (such as a business plan or articles of incorporation), and also long-term strategies. The first group of documents, shown in the upper three layers, comprises organization-level documents. The second group of documents, shown in the lower two layers, comprises operational-level documents, including the actual control measures. Each of the primary types of documents is discussed below.

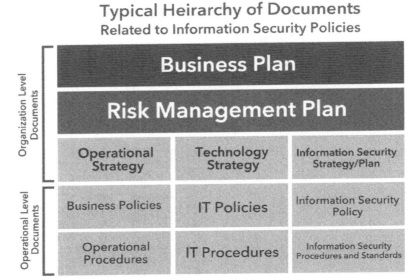

Figure 5-1. *Typical Hierarchy of Business Documents*

The intent of discussing this broader range of documents is to provide perspective on how cybersecurity governance fits into the bigger picture for the business. This will help you decide which documents, or portions of a document, would be best suited for your small business. "One size fits all" doesn't work for managing cybersecurity risks. Having a "cafeteria-style" method of selecting governance components allows you to create a custom set of documents that best meets your needs and fits the culture of your small business.

Business Governance Components – The Big Picture

We will start with the business governance components necessary for a successful cybersecurity program, which includes three organization-level documents. We will assume your business already has a business plan and a risk management plan (either together in a single document or two separate documents), so they are not described here. Some small businesses may have the content from these documents incorporated into other business documents. For example, there may be an overall business strategy that includes general business operational goals, as well as those for cybersecurity. Likewise, there may be an overall business risk management plan, which includes both business and cyber risk factors. These documents do not need to be long and complex. As a matter of fact, keeping them simple and concise (aim for no more than three pages) would be more beneficial for a small business.

The first high-level business document will be a *cybersecurity risk management plan*, which is, ideally, part of a business risk management plan. This plan describes the types and categories of cyber risk, classification of risks for each major asset, mitigation steps, and levels of acceptable risk for each major asset. As explained in Chapter 3, there are several standard methods for managing and calculating business risk. The inclusion of cyber risk will enhance the realistic, overall business risk posture.

The second high-level business document should be a *cybersecurity strategy* that includes an overall definition of the cybersecurity program. This strategy should be derived from the business plan, so that all cybersecurity efforts provide support to the business purpose and goals. The strategy can be a simple statement of the security and privacy goals for the next three to five years and outline the steps to achieve them. Refer to Appendix D for a sample template, which includes detailed components you can choose to keep or discard.

The third high-level business document is the actual *cybersecurity program* description and details. For a small business, it is recommended to include the content in the cybersecurity strategy document (refer to the template in Appendix D). The cybersecurity strategy outlines the need and direction for incorporating cybersecurity in the business, while the cybersecurity program description provides more details for an organizational program. The intent is to provide a link between the organization-level strategy and the operational-level policies and procedures. This is where the core elements of the cybersecurity program are described, such as:

- the minimum set of policies and procedures required for regulatory compliance and for maintaining an adequate level of security

- additional policies or procedures which may enhance security and reduce business risks

- a cybersecurity training and awareness program for all employees and others who have access to the business' computer systems

Below (Figure 5-2) is a different view of the business documents we've been discussing, shown from a "bottom-up" perspective, with the business plan setting the foundation for the others.

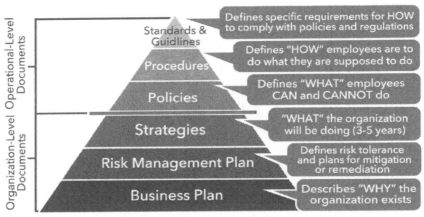

Figure 5-2. Bottom-up View of Business Documents Hierarchy

Now, let's move into the more technical aspects of the business components, which includes a few operational-level documents, as well as the actual security and privacy control measures to be implemented.

Cybersecurity policies and procedures set the direction for what employees are allowed to do or are restricted from doing. Procedures provide guidance on how to implement the policies. There are certain policies that should be considered part of the core requirements for any cybersecurity program, regardless of the level of technical complexity. We refer to this as "cyber hygiene." A list of the baseline recommended policies and procedures is provided below. Cybersecurity policies and procedures should work in concert with the business' operating policies and procedures.

Cybersecurity standards and guidelines may be used to augment the policies and procedures by providing more specific definitions and specifications. Rather than creating your own, these should be based in whole or in part on national or international standards. Start by using existing sets of standards and selecting only those that directly apply to your particular circumstances and support your policies.

To ensure the cybersecurity strategy is understood and that your employees know the relevant policies and procedures, you should have a *cybersecurity awareness and training program*. This can range from a very simple, on-the-job orientation with periodic reminders, to a full-blown series of training sessions, testing employee knowledge, and an ongoing awareness campaign. People have different modes of learning (e.g., visual, aural, interactive), so the trick is to provide the same content in different formats. Regulatory requirements may require training where you need to provide proof of completion by employees to be in compliance. Refer to the awareness and training program template in Appendix D.

A *cybersecurity incident response plan* (in concert with the disaster recovery and business continuity plans) describes the actions to be taken when a cyberattack has been discovered. This plan can be as simple as a checklist (maybe two or three pages long), or it can be more complex, with assigned roles and responsibilities and detailed procedures. Refer to examples of both types in Appendix D.

Recommended Baseline Policies and Procedures

The content of certain policies and procedures for small businesses may vary for each business based on the following characteristics:

- Industry segment/sector – primarily for those businesses in a regulated industry which specifies security requirements to be met
- Geographic dispersion of business facilities – potentially impacts physical security requirements and may affect network security between facilities
- Level and complexity of technology usage – a small office with a few desktop computers on one wired network may have different procedures than an office with a combination of desktop, laptop, and tablet computers using both wired and wireless networks
- Level of technical knowledge and expertise of the workforce –a higher level of technical expertise may allow for some more-advanced procedures
- Use of cloud services or infrastructure – requires a combination of contract terms and conditions in conjunction with company policies and procedures, specifically covering roles, responsibilities, and liabilities
- Types and volume of potentially sensitive or confidential information, including customer or client personal data – companies with sensitive or confidential data to protect may require additional security measures

There are three basic categories of security policies that should be addressed – physical security, information security, and network/systems security. All three of these categories must be coordinated and integrated with business operations and other operational policies. The following policies (and some related procedures) should be considered the baseline set needed to provide an adequate level of cyber hygiene:

Policy Title	Main Provisions
User account management	specifies how users are issued login credentials and by whom; who approves access rights for system applications and other resources; who actually creates and manages user accounts within the system; and provisions for terminating access, when necessary
Internet and email acceptable use	defines "unacceptable" and prohibited uses which would open the organization for attack; basically, restricting use of company systems for company business only; may include proactively blocking malicious websites
Protecting sensitive and confidential information	specifies steps to protect confidential information, including file, folder or full drive encryption while the information is "at rest" (stored someplace) or "in transit" (being sent across the network); also, the steps to protect confidential paper documents
Wireless access	defines when and how employees are allowed to use a wireless network connection to access the organization's computing resources; may include the use of digital certificates and a virtual private network (VPN) connection
Software updates and patch management	specifies the standard operating system version, standard business applications and web browser, and requires automatic updates for all security patches; also, a requirement to have current anti-malware software which is automatically updated
System administration security	defines who is authorized to have system administrator access, using a separate, administrative login account; requires automatic logging of all administrative actions on any of the organization's computer systems (e.g., changing the configuration settings on the email server), with log files stored separately in a location the system administrator cannot access, but where a security analyst can review them
Facility security	provides some basic requirements to keep critical computer systems secured from unauthorized physical access; employee work areas should generally be separated from areas of public access; workstations should be locked (requiring user login credentials) whenever they are unattended, and possibly shutdown after hours

Table 5-1. Baseline Policies for Cyber Hygiene

Refer to the example policies in Appendix D.

External Factors Impacting Cybersecurity Policies and Procedures

There are two primary external factors that will impact which cybersecurity policies and procedures are implemented, and the actual security controls used by any business. First, complying with regulatory requirements for your particular industry sector, whether mandated by state or federal laws or regulations. In the same category of compliance, although not state or federal legislation, is the Payment Card Industry Data Security Standards (PCI-DSS), which mandates security related to processing credit or debit card transactions. The second external factor will be the requirements placed on the business by their insurance carrier, especially if there is cybersecurity insurance coverage. Keep in mind that most compliance-related security measures should be considered as a minimum level and actually may not provide adequate levels of security to meet your own business requirements.

Technical Elements of a Cybersecurity Program

This second category of elements for the overall cybersecurity program includes security devices (hardware and software) and control measures (business procedures and practices). Cybersecurity program documents should, at a minimum:

- identify the general computing environment
- define the goals and objectives of cybersecurity measures
- define the components/elements of the cybersecurity program
- identify what set of security standards the organization is going to follow
- specify how the business plans to achieve compliance with regulatory requirements

As discussed in Section 4, using the CIS Controls falls into this category of technical elements in the cybersecurity program. Some of the sub-controls to be implemented are not really technical, per se, because they pertain to common business practices, such as maintaining an up-to-date inventory of business assets. The use of the controls will be covered later. For now, let's address several decisions and options you should consider in regard to your local office network and computers. Most of the items we are about to discuss should be documented and kept someplace safe, treated as sensitive and confidential information (e.g., kept in a locked, fire-proof cabinet), but easy to access for reference.

General computing environment: You should be familiar with your ISP service agreement, documenting what equipment they own and maintain, and what equipment they rent to you and who is responsible for its configuration settings. If there is some joint responsibility, for example setting up the primary modem/router, find out how much assistance they will provide to you and what you must do on your own. If possible, have them explain the purpose of the primary, default settings, and save a digital copy of the configuration, so it can be restored, if necessary. Be sure to change default passwords to something unique for you.

Document your office network environment: You should include an inventory of the devices in each office space (e.g., cubicle). There should be an overall strategy statement that the business has software and hardware standards, which are contained in a separate document. Inventory any peripheral devices, such as multi-function printer/copier/fax machines, and any network devices, such as wired or wireless routers with or without firewalls. If possible, create a basic network diagram showing the ISP connection coming into the office and how the various devices are connected. Figure 5-3, below, shows an example of a basic small office network.

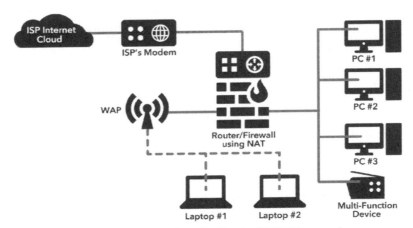

*Figure 5-3. **Example of a Basic SMB Network***

From your inventory list, you should identify the high-value assets which are critical to business operations, and then prioritize the assets from high to low. This process is described in more detail in the last chapter. Identify and document the types of security measures which should be applied to groups of similar assets. Document the level of configuration you are able to provide and maintain for the primary network devices (e.g., router and firewall), which provide some basic level of security to all devices within the network. Document the configuration settings provided by the ISP. They should leave you with sufficient documentation to know what parameters have been used for the various settings, as well as having a digital backup of the configuration settings.

The final area of the technical component will be implementing the security measures defined in the policies, procedures, and guidelines. This is where the documentation and instructions provided with the CIS Controls Implementation Group 1 (IG1) can be used as a starting point. You may also have specific internal operating procedures that you want to modify to include related cybersecurity measures.

All of this inventory and configuration documentation should be considered proprietary and confidential information and secured accordingly, including both digital and paper versions (which should be labeled with a cover page and headers or footers on each page indicating "Proprietary and Confidential Information").

Chapter 5 – Key Points and Recommended Action Items

The following is a quick summary of the key points from this chapter:

- A cybersecurity program consists of two main components – (1) a set of governance documents and (2) implementing necessary security measures and controls.
- The governance documents consist of two categories – (1) organization-level, which includes the business plan, risk management plan, and business strategies, and (2) operational-level, which includes policies, procedures, guidelines, and standards.
- The organization-level documents should incorporate the perspective and principles of cyber risk management, which will contribute to understanding and controlling overall business risk factors, inclusive of cyber risk.
- The operational-level documents related to the cybersecurity program, include cybersecurity policies and procedures covering several core topics that constitute a baseline level of security policies, and a computer security incident response plan.
- Implementing an ongoing cybersecurity awareness and training program will be a key to having a successful cybersecurity program.
- There are several steps that non-technical business owners or managers can take to implement technical aspects of a cybersecurity program without having to hire specialized cybersecurity professionals.

Here are some simple, recommended actions you can take for developing the various components of your cybersecurity program documentation:

- Use the templates provided in Appendix D to create your cybersecurity strategy, along with defining your cybersecurity program – stick to the basics of what you need and don't worry about the rest.

- Use the templates provided in Appendix D to create one overall cybersecurity policy, or create individual policies – in either case, try to maintain the core policies as a baseline; however, if something doesn't fit within your business model, then don't use it.

- In a small business, it's a good business practice to involve as many of the employees as possible during the planning stages of creating the strategy and policies; and for management to present the materials and get feedback on areas of contention or where a certain policy or procedure might impact operations negatively.

- Educate employees (and managers) on the basics of how implementing cybersecurity controls will reduce overall business risks, as long as everyone follows the policies and procedures. This can partially be related to following other workplace safety policies.

- Plan an implementation schedule that includes a review period of at least six months to evaluate the progress and success of implementing the cybersecurity program. Communicate the results to employees and conduct another feedback session.

Cybersecurity Lifecycles - They Are Processes, Not Destinations

Organizations should understand that security and privacy protection are not done once and then left in a static condition. Similar to most business functions, your security functions and cybersecurity program have ongoing lifecycles. For the overarching cybersecurity program lifecycle, the following phases would occur during implementation:

1. Define your requirements
2. Develop and initiate a strategy
3. Create policies and identify controls
4. Implement policies and controls
5. Evaluate effectiveness

Review your program annually. For your annual reviews, you will perform the following tasks:

1. Review your requirements to make sure you factor in any changes
2. Review your strategy to ensure it is still relevant to your requirements
3. Define any needed changes to policies or controls
4. Implement your changes
5. Evaluate the effectiveness of both your controls and the changes you made

   a. Program implementation
   b. Policies and controls

While it makes sense to treat your initial implementation as a project, once you get to steps 4 and 5 in the implementation list, you'll want to transition to a program that repeats the annual cycle (program review list), rather than consider the project finished. Although it's difficult to make a one-size-fits-all prediction for how long it will take to get your program in place, a good rule of thumb is four to six months for the initial program launch and then three to six weeks to conduct your annual review and make your course corrections.

Security Functions Lifecycle Process

Within the cybersecurity program, security functions have a different lifecycle, as depicted below (Figure 6-1). One main difference between the two lifecycles is that the program lifecycle is more static and scheduled annually, while the function lifecycle is more dynamic and occurs when needed. This is due to the nature of the changing threat landscape and advances in technologies for both the attackers and defenders. Generally, the five phases of the security functions lifecycle take place mostly within phase 4 of the cybersecurity program lifecycle. Phase 5 (evaluation) is common to both lifecycles, although you should evaluate the security functions before evaluating the program.

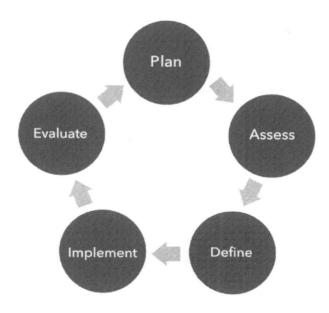

Figure 6-1. Basic Security Functions Lifecycle

The security functions lifecycle can be applied to individual assets or control measures, groups of assets or control measures, and overall assets and security measures. It's often easier to keep the groupings small – maybe ten related assets – to make the process more manageable. Each phase of the lifecycle can generally be described as these high-level tasks:

- **Plan** – this is where assets are identified, categorized, prioritized, and grouped
- **Assess** – perform a simple gap analysis of the control measures in place, existing vulnerabilities, and likely threats, then recommend additional security measures to close the gaps
- **Define** – provide configuration details for both existing and new security measures, to define how the future security state will meet business objectives and reduce risk levels

- **Implement** – put into operation the newly defined security measures
- **Evaluate** – conduct an analysis to determine how well the new security measures meet the business objectives and close the security gaps from the "Assess" phase; output from this phase is used in the next planning phase

Next, we will look at specific examples that may apply to small businesses and help you understand the lifecycle process.

Let's say that you decided your public web server is your most critical asset, based on the following assumptions:

- it is used to market and sell your products
- it is a portal for customers to place orders and make payments
- it has a link to your separate customer service database server, only available to authorized employees, not the public
- if the web server were not available or if its data became corrupted, it would have a major impact on your business
- depending on how long it takes to bring it back online and functioning properly, the result could be the total loss of the business (if not restored quickly enough)

Next, we'll walk through the security functions lifecycle for this asset, as an example of the steps to take at each phase, which can then be extrapolated to other assets and the business as a whole.

Example Steps for Each Lifecycle Phase

The *planning phase* ideally starts when you decide to implement a web server and before it is placed into operation. In today's world, you will most likely use hosted web services through a CSP rather than purchase a server. Planning should start when the CSP makes a hosted web server available and includes the identification of all of the attributes of the asset – in the case of our example, we have these assumptions:

- it's a publicly available web server
- it hosts information about your business and your products or services
- it's also a transaction portal for customers to place orders and make payments
- the actual customer information is stored on a separate database server
- the financial transactions are managed on a separate, secure server
- no personal or financial information is stored on the web server

Next, you will need to answer some questions: Who is going to manage the server (ensuring the operating system and web server software are kept updated)? Who is going to manage the web site (the "look and feel" of your business, keeping the content updated)? Who will maintain the web applications (customer interface for making purchases and payments)? These questions need to be answered during planning because they either impact the security of the server directly or at least who will be responsible for different aspects of security. Another consideration is whether or not you want to have a second (backup) web server for redundancy in case the primary server goes offline, or possibly for compliance with regulatory requirements.

In the *assess phase* for your web server, the answers to the planning questions should guide the assumptions about what security measures you will need to implement, and what security measures will be provided by others (e.g., CSP or ISP). During this phase, there are two types of assessments to perform. First, there is a pre-deployment threat analysis to identify known potential threats to web servers. Then, during deployment, you implement appropriate security measures to mitigate those threats. Second, there should be a vulnerability assessment to determine any security gaps which may be used as targets of an attack. Keep in mind that we are just using a web server as an example. In reality, you will want to work through this process for each group of similar assets at the same time.

Another analysis tool that is becoming more common is creating a threat model. This takes into account vulnerabilities, known threats, and mitigating security measures. To fully identify the risks, the threat model helps depict as many attack scenarios as possible. This activity is something that would be done by a professional team, working in conjunction with the small business. In addition to the threat modeling, you will also want your vendor to perform a basic analysis of vulnerabilities that might affect your environment. They will use a combination of tools for general system vulnerability assessments and for testing web sites and applications. These tools will automatically indicate a high, medium, or low criticality level, and you will work with them to use a risk matrix to help assign an overall risk value to each critical asset. Prioritize those assets with high risk scores to be remediated first. Should you choose to do this yourself or take this in-house once the initial review has been done, there are several free software tools available for this purpose.

Let's look at some examples of vulnerabilities for web servers and potential solutions:

Vulnerability	Mitigation (Solution)
Invalid or expired digital certificate (used to validate the authenticity of your web site)	Acquire and install a new, valid certificate (usually good for 3-5 years)
Out-of-date web server software (e.g., IIS or Apache)	Setup regular, ongoing updates as part of a patch management process
Invalid configuration or missing security protocol (i.e., using HTTP instead of HTTPS)	Ensure proper use of Secure Socket Layer (SSL) protocol or other web security protocols
Server firewall not enabled	Enable the server's firewall and configure authorized access; use a "block all" default setting and create an Access Control List (ACL) for authorized users
Server anti-malware signatures are out of date	Configure the anti-malware software to automatically download and install updated signature files daily
Data entry fields without data validation checks (e.g., numeric data fields should not accept any non-numeric entries)	Set the data validation parameters for each field to prevent invalid entries
Unused ports are open on the server	Only ports being used for specific services or protocols should be open, all other ports should be closed and unavailable for access

Table 6-1. Example Vulnerabilities and Solutions

Keep in mind that some of these examples may require your ISP or CSP to take action, based on who is managing the server infrastructure and the type of service being provided.

Now that you know the areas of weakness, the ***define phase*** is used to create a detailed plan of action and specific countermeasures that are needed. In coordination with your ISP or CSP, you document the security controls you will provide and configure and the ones they are responsible for providing. If possible, you should have a written agreement with any third-party service provider that specifically defines responsibilities and liabilities for both overall services and specifically for security matters. Some ISPs and CSPs provide basic security as part of the core contract but require you to pay for more advanced security services. Work with a consultant or MSSP (managed security services provider), as needed, to ensure that your web server's operating system, software, website content, and web application for the customer interface are all properly secured. Your ISP or CSP would likely ensure that the network security, routine data backups, and possibly a digital security certificate are all maintained and up to date.

The *implement phase* puts into operation the security measures you have worked on up to this point. Small businesses usually do not have the luxury of having a separate test environment and must implement new systems or make configuration changes to their production (operational) computers and network. You should have an implementation plan for your web server. The plan should address how to test its functionality to make sure it operates as expected, including interfaces with other systems and all of the integrated security measures. When implementing several changes, don't do them all at once — do one at a time, testing to ensure the change functions as planned, then move on to the next. The plan should contain contingencies for reverting to the prior state if something major fails. You might need to "back out" just the most recent change or all of the changes. The plan should also have some success milestones — such as properly reporting security alarms or operating for one week or one month without any system failures caused by the security measures.

The *evaluate phase* does not have a fixed duration and is dependent on the number, types, and complexity of changes or additions that were made to the computing environment. Each separate component can have different timing to complete an evaluation — some may last for one month, and others may take six months. Of course, you will be looking at all of your critical systems and applications, not just the web server used as an example. Actually, once all systems are up and running smoothly, this process becomes ongoing throughout the year. You might want to schedule some more formalized evaluations on a quarterly or semi-annual basis, to have documentation for the next planning cycle.

Since this whole process is related to security functions, the focus is on which controls or security measures were implemented and how effective they have been. In addition, you should conduct periodic vulnerability assessments to find any "new" security gaps that need to be mitigated. There will be different interpretations of effectiveness, depending on what has occurred over the evaluation period. In addition to effectiveness measures, there are other performance measures at the operational level, and some administrative measures of interest at the management level.

First, you need to set the goals to be achieved – these could be weekly, monthly, quarterly, or annually. As long as they are well-defined, the goals may relate either to a particular asset (e.g., primary web server) or more broadly for the company (e.g., awareness training). Success or effectiveness is measured by how well the goals are met – reporting that you had no security breaches or system compromises is good news. For the purpose of this example, a "breach" would involve unauthorized access to a system without any data loss or damage. A "system compromise" would involve unauthorized access where data was stolen or deleted, or your systems' settings were modified. In reporting there were no breaches in a month it makes a difference if you can show that your systems were never targeted with an attack. In the case of reporting no system compromises in a month, it makes a difference that your security measures blocked dozens of attacks. In this second case, you know that your security measures were successful and effective; however, in the first case, there is no way to know if they would have blocked an attack. Don't be discouraged by this. The point is that you didn't have a data breach or system compromise.

After all of the evaluations are complete, the documentation is used to inform the next planning phase and the cycle starts over, even if you don't need to make any major changes. The intent of repeating the cybersecurity program lifecycle each year is to foster continuous improvement in your security posture. The intent of repeating the security functions lifecycle as needed is staying up with current threats and vulnerabilities. The final results of the security functions lifecycle process should be used as input into the planning phase of the program lifecycle.

Chapter 6 – Key Points and Recommended Action Items

The following is a quick summary of the key points from this chapter:

- There are two different lifecycles for the cybersecurity program and for cybersecurity functions, both of which need to be ongoing, usually on an annual cycle for the program and on an as-needed basis for the functions.
- The five phases of the cybersecurity program lifecycle are: (1) define/refine security requirements, (2) develop and initiate a cybersecurity strategy, (3) create policies and identify appropriate security controls, (4) implement the policies and controls, and (5) evaluate the effectiveness of the program implementation.
- The five phases of the cybersecurity functions lifecycle are independent of the program lifecycle and consist of: (1) Plan, (2) Assess, (3) Define, (4) Implement, and (5) Evaluate.
- While the program lifecycle evaluation is conducted for the whole organization, the security functions steps and phases are performed on small groups of similar assets that have been prioritized (high risk and high value).
- The planning phase of the security functions lifecycle is a critical first step that provides the groundwork for the other phases.

Here are some recommended action items to help you conduct an assessment using the security functions lifecycle:

- For the *planning phase*, identify your critical assets, group them by similarity of usage, prioritize them for high value, then determine roles and responsibilities for providing security for each high priority asset.
- For the *assess phase*, you need to know who is responsible for providing security; the responsible party then performs a

vulnerability assessment on groups of high priority assets under their control. This action assumes that all applicable assets are already deployed and in use.

- For the ***define phase***, use the results of the assessments to determine the gaps in existing security measures to protect against attacks aimed at the found vulnerabilities; create a plan to implement needed security controls to close the gaps, which may be the responsibility of the CSP or ISP.

- For the ***implement phase***, use a phased approach to only implement one change at a time and create a safe restore point after each successful change. Have a contingency plan to revert back to a prior operational state if changes fail or cause system errors.

- For the ***evaluate phase***, set a review time period, usually three months after changes are implemented, and evaluate the success and effectiveness of the changes. This evaluation could show the results of the security measures by having no successful attacks against your systems and the number of attempted attacks that were blocked. The specific measures will depend on the goals that were set.

Chapter 7

Incorporating Privacy Requirements with Cybersecurity

Many people think that when they implement appropriate security measures, they have met the needs of consumers' privacy. Security serves a purpose in meeting some privacy requirements for keeping a customer's personal information secure. You often hear the phrase, "You can have security without privacy, but you can't have privacy without security." Think of security as covering the basics, which may not be   sufficient for privacy. Security plays a key role in most privacy regulations. Those regulations provide protections for consumers' rights regarding what personal information they provide to an organization. The regulations govern how that information is used and how it must be protected. They also cover the consumers' right to know what is done with their information and the right to "opt out" of having any of their information kept by the organization, without discrimination.

On the business side, companies must provide mechanisms that allow consumers to manage their personal information – collection, storage, use or handling, sharing, and deletion. In the same way that cybersecurity measures should enable secure business operations, they should also enable consumer privacy through secure data management. Do you, as a small business, need to be concerned about consumer privacy rights, even if there might be an exception in one of the laws? Yes, you should be concerned about the personal information you collect from customers since that data will make you a target for cybercriminals.

There are numerous privacy laws that impact business today, but we will discuss three primary laws and their possible impact on your business. The first one is commonly known by its acronym, "GDPR," which stands for General Data Protection Regulation, enacted in April 2016 by the Council of the European Union. You might be thinking, "Why should I be concerned with a European regulation for my small business in the USA?" Keep reading and find out! The second one is the California Consumer Privacy Act of 2018 (or "CCPA"). Again, you might ask, "My small business is in another state, why does this concern me?" The third set of laws that are relevant to privacy are contained within the Federal Trade Commission Act (or "FTCA") (Title 16 U.S. Code). The FTC has been in the business of consumer protection for nearly a century, and privacy is just one aspect of their jurisdiction. These questions will be addressed as we discuss the three laws; however, keep in mind that the focus of this chapter is how to incorporate as many of the privacy requirements into your cybersecurity program as possible. We will not be discussing the details of implementing a privacy program. There are books and training videos created specifically to cover privacy, and you might want to consult with an attorney regarding your small business being compliant with relevant privacy laws.

Before looking into these three sets of laws and regulations, the underlying purpose of privacy protections can be summarized in the following seven principles. These are derived and paraphrased from Recital 39 of the GDPR. (Note that the term "consumer" is used here, while the GDPR refers to a "natural person.")

- The collection, storage, processing, use, and dissemination of personal information must be transparent, legal, and fair. ("Dissemination" includes the sale of information.)
- The organization collecting, storing, processing, using, or disseminating personal information must provide the consumer with three pieces of information, in clear, easily understood language:

- o   the nature of information being requested
- o   the purpose for which it will be used
- o   clearly identify the organization that is requesting and maintaining the information.

- Consumers have the right to request confirmation from an organization regarding what personal information has been collected about them and how it is being used or processed.

- Organizations must be transparent in making the consumer aware of their rights and the risks, rules, and safeguards related to processing and use of personal information, and how to exercise their rights.

- The personal information requested and collected should be relevant, adequate, and limited to the specific purpose for which it is requested. The purpose should be explicit and legitimate at the time the request is made.

- Time limits should be set for the retention of personal information. It should be kept only as long as legitimately necessary, and then properly deleted. Inaccurate or outdated information should be corrected or deleted as quickly as possible.

- Collection, storage, processing, or use of personal information must be done in a manner that ensures the confidentiality and security of personal data. The personal data must be protected against unauthorized access.

Why Should You Be Aware of and Understand the GDPR?

Your U.S.-based, local, small business may not be required to comply with the GDPR; however, having a basic understanding of its privacy requirements may still benefit your small business. There might come a time when your business does become subject to GDPR requirements due to a change in your customers or in your business model. There is a strong likelihood that future legislation in one or more states within the U.S. will mirror GDPR requirements. In fact, the CCPA (summarized below) is similar to Articles 12 to 20 of the GDPR, covering the rights of the data subject (consumer). The basic tenets of the GDPR include the following:

- There are special conditions for organizations with less than 250 employees, and direction is given to EU nations to take into account the special needs of micro, small, and medium-sized businesses.

- The GDPR applies to the protection of natural persons (consumers) and the free movement of personal data within the internal (EU) market, to provide consistent legal rights for consumers across the national jurisdictions. The GDPR does not apply to "legal persons," which could be a business entity, such as a partnership.

- The GDPR applies to both automated and manual processing of personal data, and protections should be technology-neutral (not based on a particular proprietary system).

- The GDPR principles and rules must be applied consistently, "to provide a strong and coherent protection framework."

- The GDPR applies to commercial and professional activities and does not apply to personal or household activities, which includes keeping addresses for correspondence or social networking. However, the GDPR applies to controller or processor companies who provide the means for processing the data for personal or household activities.

Where does this all lead for your small business? The GDPR sets up a core set of privacy expectations, the primary one being that the data subject (consumer) has ownership over their data and a right to have a direct and active role in how their information is used. U.S.-based small businesses can use this as a general guideline, rather than a mandate.

What Should You Know about the CCPA?

Whether your small business is located in California or any other state, if you have customers who are residents of California then this law might apply to you. The California Consumer Privacy Act of 2018 (CCPA), as amended, is applicable to businesses that meet any one of these criteria:

- has gross annual revenue of greater than $25 million
- buys, receives, sells, or shares the personal information of 50,000 or more consumers, households, or devices annually
- derives 50% or more of annual income from selling consumers' personal information

By way of example, if your small business were to meet any of these criteria, it's likely that you might exceed the second threshold. A simple mathematical formula shows that if you have an average of just 137 credit card transactions per day, you will reach the 50,000-transaction annual threshold ($137 \times 365 = 50,005$).

Even if the CCPA doesn't directly apply to your small business, it can be beneficial for you to understand the provisions. This way, you can implement necessary safeguards and show that you have done your due diligence in protecting and managing your customers' personal information. The core requirements of the CCPA include:

- Organizations must post a privacy policy on their website.
- Organizations must notify consumers of the specific personal information that is being requested and saved. They must also disclose the purpose for which the organization will use that information. Such uses may include sharing the information "internally" with affiliates of the host organization, sharing it with other third-party businesses, or selling the information.
- Ideally, any data collection of personal information from consumers should use an "opt-in" method, which means no

information is automatically required or collected, and that the consumer elects to provide only the information they want to provide. This is counter to the popular "opt-out" method, which collects personal information from the consumer by default and requires the consumer to select an opt-out option in order for the personal information to not be collected or saved.

- Once a consumer has elected to opt in, the organization must provide an easy mechanism for them to opt out at any time. The organization cannot discriminate against the consumer for opting out. Also, opting out cannot impact the terms and conditions or the consumer's relationship with the organization.

Understanding the FTC's Consumer Privacy Requirements

The Federal Trade Commission (FTC) has broad regulatory powers to protect consumers from "unfair and deceptive" trade practices. The FTC has a long history of enforcement actions. Many of their case summaries are available on their website at *https://www.ftc.gov/enforcement/cases-proceedings*.

Under the Federal Trade Commission   Act (FTCA), all businesses must not use or participate in any unfair methods of competition related to commerce (i.e., business transactions), and also any other unfair or deceptive acts or practices which affect commerce.

As stated earlier, cybersecurity measures need to support and enable compliance with privacy requirements. While not specifically identified in the FTCA, in general this means the following security measures or features would help ensure that a small business is not using unfair business practices:

- All Personally Identifiable Information (PII), Personal Health Information (PHI), Payment Card Information

(PCI), and any other confidential or sensitive information should be adequately protected while at rest (stored/saved on a server) and while in transit (transmitted across a network). As an example, there are four or five potential methods of securing data within a database.

- Physical protection must be used when confidential information is displayed or viewed on a computer screen, as well as for printed documents. This means using monitor screen filters or other means of preventing an unauthorized bystander from viewing a computer screen without being directly in front of it. It also means blocking the viewing of printed materials and locking them in a cabinet when they are not being used.

- Authorization for access to any confidential information should follow the principle of least privilege and must be approved by an appropriate manager or executive. This principle means that a person is given the least amount of access rights or privileges that are necessary to perform their job functions, and no more.

- Access rights through an automated system must be controlled so that only properly authorized individuals can access the information. Authorization approvals should be reviewed and renewed at least annually. When an authorized individual changes their job role or leaves the organization, it should trigger an automatic revocation of their access rights. If their new role within the organization requires access to confidential information, they must be re-approved by the authorizing manager.

- Security mechanisms that ensure the protection of the data that is stored by an organization must also provide the means for data to be deleted completely from all saved versions (i.e., the master database and all backup copies). This feature is necessary to comply with the current laws for a consumer who elects to opt out of having their information saved or used by an organization.

The FTC has issued several major consent decrees related to privacy on the grounds of unfair or deceptive business practices. These include well-known companies, such as PayPal, Microsoft, Amazon, and Facebook. Each year, the FTC investigates several consumer information breaches and dictates the terms and conditions under which businesses can continue to operate and how they are required to manage and protect consumer information.

Privacy Requirements Differ from Cybersecurity

Now, let's recap what you should understand about privacy and how cybersecurity measures are not the same as privacy controls. The main theme across the laws we have reviewed is that the consumer maintains ownership of their personal information and has the right to control what information is collected about them and how that information is used, and has the ability to opt out, such that their information is fully deleted. Organizations that collect and manage consumers' personal information must protect it from unauthorized access and provide mechanisms for the consumer to self-manage their personal information held by the organization. Even if your small business technically falls outside of the scope of existing laws, it would be beneficial to follow the security and privacy requirements, which would help lower business risk and probably reduce your liability.

Chapter 7 – Key Points and Recommended Action Items

The following is a quick summary of the key points from this chapter:

- Cybersecurity measures should enable and support compliance with privacy regulations by providing secure data management.

- While cybersecurity measures are meant to keep personal data secure, privacy requirements focus on the customers' rights to determine what information they share and how and with whom their information is shared, and the consumer's ability to opt out at any time.

- Three primary privacy laws are applicable – the General Data Protection Regulation (GDPR) for the European Union, the California Consumer Privacy Act of 2018 (CCPA), and the Federal Trade Commission Act (FTCA), all as amended. Similar laws are in the process of being enacted in states across the U.S. and in other countries.

- Organizations must disclose what personal information they are gathering or maintaining, and its specific purpose (how it is being used). Consumers have the right to limit what personal information they provide and, to a certain extent, restrict its use by an organization.

- Organizations must have a legitimate and relevant purpose for which they are collecting personal information, which must be disclosed at the time the personal information is requested. Automatic data collection should not be the default – organizations should allow the consumer to opt in before collecting personal information.

- Security and protection of personal data applies to both digital and paper copies, and to both manual and automated processes.

- Organizations need to make their privacy policy readily available and, pursuant to the CCPA, have it posted on their website.

- Organizations must provide clear instructions for consumers to opt out of providing any personal information. Further, if a consumer wants to have their personal information removed from an organization's records, the organization must provide a means for making such a request and the technical capability to ensure that all of the related personal information is deleted, including from backups.

- Access to an organization's stored personal data from its customers must be controlled and limited only to authorized employees and should follow the principle of least privilege access rights. Authorized access should be restricted to those job roles which require access to perform their duties.

- Organizations that use personal information from consumers in such a manner as to create unfair competition with other organizations or for conducting any unfair or deceptive business practices may be subject to sanctions and fines.

Here are some simple actions you can take to integrate privacy requirements into a cybersecurity program for your small business:

- Understand the general requirements related to consumer privacy rights, and the specific requirements for those laws that directly apply to your small business. Seek the assistance of a privacy professional if necessary.

- Research free information related to privacy policies and create your own privacy policy. If your attorney didn't help create the policy, have it reviewed by an attorney before publishing it to ensure it complies with any applicable laws.

- From a cybersecurity perspective, ensure that adequate and necessary security controls and procedures are implemented to protect consumer personal information, both "at rest" (stored/saved on a server) and "in transit" (transmitted across a network).

- Ensure that clear instructions and tools are in place for your customers to understand their privacy rights and for taking action to exercise those rights; provide methods to allow "out-of-band" actions (i.e., for telephone or mail service).

- Ensure that your internal procedures only allow authorized employees to have access to consumer personal information, only at the level of detail required for their jobs, following the principle of least privilege.

Step-by-step Guide to Building Your Cybersecurity Plan

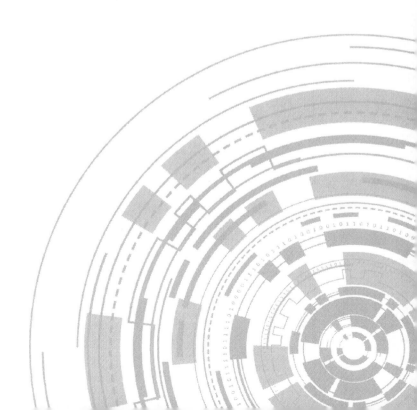

> "When I am out speaking about cybersecurity, the most frequent, and often the most earnest and heart-felt question that I hear is 'Where do I begin?' This is the problem that IG1 takes on - to remove the wizardry and fog of cybersecurity, and help people take the most important foundational first steps of improvement."
>
> Tony Sager, Executive Vice President & Controls Evangelist, CIS

This section will outline the basic steps to take in creating a cybersecurity program. These steps, as detailed in Chapters 8, 9, and 10, will walk you through completing the templates in Appendix D for developing a set of customized documents. Appendix D provides the online link where you can download the template files. Several of the resources for small businesses listed in Appendix B also have helpful templates and example documents available; we will refer to some of these at appropriate points in our discussion.

The order of the steps in this section exposes the elements of the program template in a way that makes it a little easier to construct your customized program. The steps we will discuss don't line up directly with the program sections, but the finished product will have all of the components you need in the right order.

Developing a Small Business Cybersecurity Strategy

We covered an introduction on the topic of cybersecurity strategy back in Chapter 5, as we looked at the overview of governance documents. Looking at the bottom-up approach, the foundation of the pyramid consists of the business plan and risk management plan, followed by business strategies. These three layers comprise the organization-level documents, which means they provide the overarching direction (or underlying foundation) for all aspects of the business. As you can deduce, a cybersecurity strategy falls into this area and will guide the other, operational-level cybersecurity documents.

A cybersecurity strategy is intended to articulate management's goals and objectives for the following three to five years, as well as define an ongoing cybersecurity program. The strategy document is usually not very long, as some of the details will be contained in other governance documents. It should define the various roles and responsibilities related to IT and cybersecurity management and operations. In a small business, one person will likely be responsible for the duties of several roles. It is also likely that some of the more technical duties are obtained through contract services, either on an ongoing basis or through ad hoc, as-needed services.

The purpose of this chapter is to provide definitions for the component sections within the cybersecurity strategy document. The actions from this chapter will guide you in creating a working draft version of a strategy and basic cybersecurity program. These draft documents will be further developed and completed by following the steps in Chapters 9 and 10. During this process of starting to define your strategy, it is a best practice to involve your employees in discussions about the purpose and goals of having a cybersecurity strategy and ongoing program. At some point, these employee discussions should also include the creation of policies and procedures.

Depending on your particular small business and the skill sets of your employees and their involvement with designing processes and procedures, it might be beneficial to create employee teams to work on creating draft versions of certain sections of the strategy and program documents. For example, one team might develop the cybersecurity awareness and training program, while another team works on the business continuity and disaster recovery plans, and a third team creates the incident response procedures. Employee acceptance and support will be important factors in the successful implementation of the cybersecurity program.

A basic cybersecurity strategy document contains the following sections, which apply to businesses of all sizes.

The Components of the Cybersecurity Program	
Program Section	**Description**
1.0	Management Commitment
2.0	Purpose and Goals
3.0	Strategy Statement
4.0	Creation of a Cybersecurity Program
	4.1 Roles and Responsibilities
	4.2 Minimum Information Security Policies and Procedures
	4.3 Use of Standardized Security Controls
	4.4 Cybersecurity Awareness amd Training Program
5.0	Emergency Management Planning for Cybersecurity
	5.1 Business Continuity Plan
	5.2 Disaster Recovery Plan
6.0	Cybersecurity Incident Response Plan
7.0	Regular Review of Cybersecurity Strategy and Cybersecurity Program

The specific level of detail will be more limited for small businesses.

An overview of each section is discussed below to help you use the template provided in Appendix D to create your own, customized strategy document. More details for each section are discussed in the next two chapters.

Management Commitment – this is a simple statement, accompanied by the signature of the CEO or President, that affirmatively states management's commitment to the cybersecurity strategy and cybersecurity program.

Purpose and Goals – this section provides the primary purpose and specific goals for the strategy. An example of a purpose for the strategy would be to ensure the adequate protection of the organization's information assets, including confidential customer information, through the structured implementation of standardized security controls. An example of a strategic goal would be the implementation of the cybersecurity program, including related policies and procedures and a cybersecurity awareness and training program, within a stated time frame (e.g., six months after approving the strategy).

Strategy Statement – this should be a simple, goal-oriented statement about management's strategic direction for the use of cybersecurity controls. This element should provide the overarching direction for the purpose and goals. For example:

> "Over the next three years, it is *ABC Company*'s strategy to implement an appropriate set of cybersecurity controls, to reduce overall business risk and provide adequate levels of cybersecurity to achieve the goal of having no cyberattacks where data loss or destruction occurs. This strategy relies on the successful implementation of a cybersecurity program, with its associated policies, procedures, and employee training."

Creation of a Cybersecurity Program – this section and its related subsections should provide a clear statement of management's intent to implement and maintain necessary and adequate security measures by creating an ongoing cybersecurity program. This is where each of the major components are defined, including:

- the assignment of roles and responsibilities for cybersecurity tasks to specific job functions
- listing the core set of policies and procedures, with the ability to add others without having to modify the strategy document
- a declaration of the published security standards that will be used by your small business
- the definition of a cybersecurity awareness and training program

Ideally, the number of available employees or managers exceeds the number of roles to be filled, although, in reality, each staff person usually fills more than one role. Most small businesses have very few or no staff dedicated to IT functions, let alone to cybersecurity. Typically, one or two employees have a knack for technology and end up filling the "IT support" role and, by extension, the cybersecurity roles. The downside of this type of organizational model is that these employees often do not have the necessary training or experience to be truly effective in those roles. However, it is better to have someone with minimal skills filling those roles, rather than no one.

Having a defined program where expectations are known in advance will help an organization perform monitoring to detect and protect against threats or compromises, and during the response and recovery phases of a cyberattack. The program also provides a framework and guidance to the organization by defining roles and responsibilities, using well-known standards, and setting security goals and objectives. These aspects of cybersecurity work together to reduce overall business risk levels.

Emergency Management Planning for Cybersecurity – this section should be an extension of other business planning documents, specifically for disaster recovery (DR) and business continuity (BC). Basically, cyber risks should be addressed along with other business risks that could impact operations, including floods, fires, earthquakes, and tornados. First and foremost, these plans should address the safety of employees and other people who may be located at the offices or other facilities of your small business. After ensuring physical safety, then it's a matter of prioritizing business functions and operations.

You should be able to use the prioritized list of computing assets developed as part of your inventory and risk assessment to determine which assets would need to remain in operation, at some minimal level, for the business to remain open and operational. Before making any operational decisions, ensure that the surrounding infrastructure (e.g., power, water, and other utilities) is also functioning. If the necessary physical and human assets are available, the BCP (business continuity plan) would take effect. If the minimal business functions cannot be made operational, then the business should use the DRP (disaster recovery plan) to start preparing for the restoration of basic operations.

Depending on the nature, scope, and cause of an emergency incident or disaster, the steps to be taken for either the BCP or DRP will vary for cyber-related events versus other disasters. In all cases, the first priority is the safety of all staff and visitors, followed by the protection of critical assets. Organizations with redundant systems, regular file backups, and proper security measures in place are more likely to be able to use the BCP to get core operations restarted quickly and restore full operations more easily.

Cybersecurity Incident Response Plan – this section defines the creation of an incident response plan to be used for response to and recovery from a cyberattack. The actual incident response plan is a separate document. The cybersecurity strategy should identify key roles and responsibilities for developing and executing the incident response plan. This is a critical component of the cybersecurity program, because failure to respond correctly to a cyberattack may result in a business (small or medium size) going out of business. In addition, the response procedures and processes can "make or break" a criminal investigation by properly identifying and preserving evidence, which may also be necessary for filing an insurance claim or for proving compliance with regulatory requirements.

This response plan should explain how and where employees should report suspicious computer activity or instances when they think their computer might have been compromised. The awareness and training program should teach employees how to recognize a potential cyberattack, so they know what to report. For a small business, the response plan itself can be just a simple set of instructions that accompany a checklist of response and recovery items. For regulated businesses, there might be requirements for a more detailed response plan, which basically includes additional details about each potential and actual incident. The level of reporting detail may or may not change the actions that need to be taken to stop an attack and mitigate its effects. In addition, for those incidents where a data breach has actually occurred, the plan should address notification requirements based on the applicable state laws.

This section of the overall cybersecurity strategy and program should outline the level of detail and type of reporting, which is required, either internally or for compliance reasons. It might also divide cyberattacks into categories of severity, which are then applied in the response plan as different priorities or modes of response. For example, an attack against your primary website might be severity level 1 (high priority), whereas finding a single instance of malware on one laptop might be severity level 3 (medium-low priority).

Regular Review of Cybersecurity Strategy and Cybersecurity Program – this final section should identify the scope and frequency for management to review the strategy (annually) and the program (annually or every six months). The strategic review remains at a high level with a three-year planning horizon. The program review should include more details and often involves a review of current controls, a vulnerability assessment, threat model, and gap analysis (to identify where security controls are not addressing vulnerabilities). You should also be reviewing the effectiveness of the cybersecurity awareness and training program at least annually.

Chapter 8 – Key Points and Recommended Action Items

The following is a quick summary of the key points from this chapter:

- Creating a cybersecurity strategy aligned with your business plan is the first step in developing a cybersecurity program for your small business – it sets the foundation for operational policies and procedures.
- Use the outline with seven major topic headings. Your cybersecurity strategy can be as simple or as complex as you want it to be, consistent with your small business culture. Each heading should be addressed, at least to a minimal extent. In Chapters 9 and 10, we will walk through the process of creating customized documents.
- In describing the cybersecurity program, you can use this strategy document to contain the full description or use it to provide an overview of the program and describe it more fully in a separate document.
- Planning ahead for emergencies is a key factor in having a successful recovery of business operations, so put time into creating a BCP and a DRP, as separate from your cybersecurity strategy.

Here are some recommended action items to help you begin to formulate your own, customized cybersecurity strategy, including the creation of a cybersecurity program:

- Get your management team together to create your cybersecurity strategy statement, along with a purpose and goals, ensuring that all are aligned with your business plan and company's mission statement.
- Start working with the templates from Appendix D to create working draft versions of a cybersecurity strategy and cybersecurity program definition. These will be completed in Chapters 9 and 10.

Chapter 9

Defining the Cybersecurity Strategy, Policy, and Standards

This chapter will outline the ten basic steps to take in creating a cybersecurity program. We will bring together what you have already completed and summarize what has been presented up to this point. These steps, combined with Chapter 10, will walk you through completing the templates in Appendix D for developing a set of customized documents. Appendix D provides the online link where you can download the template files. Several of the resources for small businesses listed in Appendix B also have templates and example documents available.

The first four steps below will guide you through creating your cybersecurity strategy and crafting your program. This includes drafting your policies and selecting the controls you'll need to meet your policy requirements. In Chapter 10, the remaining six steps will help you develop some of the essential operating mechanisms to manage your program.

- Step 1 – Create a cybersecurity strategy
- Step 2 – Define and implement an overarching cybersecurity program
- Step 3 – Create cybersecurity policies and procedures (keeping privacy in mind)
- Step 4 – Select a standard set of security controls to meet policy requirements

These actions primarily set up the governance structure for your cybersecurity program, and Section 5 will address the beginning stages of actually implementing some basic security measures. Some of the CIS Sub-Controls in "Implementation Group 1" (IG1) involve setting up a governance structure with policies and procedures. Where applicable, the action items in the steps below indicate which Sub-Control is being met by completing the action. Using the template in Appendix D will provide some flexibility to make updates more frequently than if the cybersecurity strategy were incorporated into other business strategies; although, you are free to integrate your business and cybersecurity strategies. Throughout the process of creating your cybersecurity program, the management team should work collaboratively and involve the employees as much as possible (at least to get feedback), to gain the greatest buy-in for the program.

Step 1: Create a cybersecurity strategy

This organization-level governance document provides the cybersecurity strategy for the business over a three- to five-year period. In this step, we focus on completing the first three sections of the template, while the other sections (displaying the outline we introduced in the section intro below for easy reference) are addressed in subsequent steps.

The Components of the Cybersecurity Program

Program Section	Description
1.0	Management Commitment
2.0	Purpose and Goals
3.0	Strategy Statement
4.0	Creation of a Cybersecurity Program
	4.1 Roles and Responsibilities
	4.2 Minimum Information Security Policies and Procedures
	4.3 Use of Standardized Security Controls
	4.4 Cybersecurity Awareness amd Training Program
5.0	Emergency Management Planning for Cybersecurity
	5.1 Business Continuity Plan
	5.2 Disaster Recovery Plan
6.0	Cybersecurity Incident Response Plan
7.0	Regular Review of Cybersecurity Strategy and Cybersecurity Program

Use the template from Appendix D to craft your own cybersecurity strategy. Complete sections 1.0, 2.0, and 3.0 by modifying any of the wording to make it fit your particular business. You may also add anything you think is relevant to your business, for example, how this strategy links with and supports your business plan.

Develop an "all-hazards" emergency management plan that includes a business continuity plan and a disaster recovery plan, covering acts of nature (e.g., flood, tornado or hurricane, pandemic, fire, and earthquake) and man-made disasters (e.g., arson fires, corporate sabotage, cyberattacks, vandalism, and theft). [CIS Control 19.1]

Step 2: Define and implement an overarching cybersecurity program

The cybersecurity program includes people (roles and responsibilities), processes (policies, procedures, standards, and guidelines), and technologies (security controls), aligned with and supporting business operations and functions. In this step, we focus on the people aspect.

- Continue using the template from Appendix D, which was started in step 1 above, to complete sections 4.0 and 4.1. Review the functions and responsibilities for each role (job position) and determine whether each one is performed by someone in your small business or by your ISP or CSP, or if no one currently performs the function. [CIS Control 19.1]
- Separate out the roles performed by you and your employees and identify in the document which of your job functions perform each of the applicable roles. Often in a small business, one position performs several roles; however, be cautious about assigning responsibilities beyond the scope and abilities of any one position. [CIS Control 19.3]
- Investigate which of the remaining roles and responsibilities are performed by your ISP or CSP. Inform the service providers that you are creating a cybersecurity program and discuss how they can support you through the existing contracts for the functions that fall within their scope.
- For any remaining responsibilities that are not covered by your staff or the ISP or CSP, decide whether you want to leave them unassigned, assign them to existing roles, or seek assistance from the ISP or CSP.
- In some cases, after a breach, you may also be able to request assistance from local law enforcement or the FBI; however, there are minimum requirements that must be met in regard to the nature and extent of the breach and resulting losses or costs to the organization. In many cases, the local law

enforcement agency or FBI will offer advice, but not handle the breach recovery tasks.

Step 3: Create cybersecurity policies and procedures

This step involves completing section 4.2 in the strategy template and also completing the separate policy template. You can determine how to organize the policies – it may be appropriate to have one policy document with a section for each topic, or you may want a short policy document for each topic. In Appendix D, the template provides one policy document containing each topic, from which you can select and customize each policy for your particular small business. If you plan to create separate policies for each topic, you should maintain consistency with the header block, and you will need to have a purpose, scope, and definitions for each policy.

These core policies are recommended as the minimum set of policies for any organization; however, there may be one or more of these policies that do not apply to your small business – simply remove them. Similarly, there may be other policies that do apply to your particular circumstances but are not part of the template in Appendix D. If that is the case, check the resources in Appendix B for potential templates to adapt to your purpose.

This is a good place to point out a potential area of contention between management's policies and employees' expectation of privacy at work. Within the Internet and Email Acceptable Use Policy, there is a section that states management's right to monitor all computer activity on company-owned computers and networks, and also on authorized, private devices which are accessing company servers and networks. This policy includes a statement of acknowledgment which employees must sign, confirming that they understand they are to have no expectation of privacy in regard to computer and network activity when using company computing resources. The purpose of monitoring these resources is to watch for anomalous or malicious activity, and not to spy on employees. Only authorized security staff are allowed to review the activity log files or view the active network monitoring tools. General supervisors and managers should not be given access to any employee computer activity without having an independent reason to investigate a specific violation of work rules or other documented performance issues. This is usually a hot topic item for discussion during the "All Hands" meeting (see Chapter 10).

In some cases, depending on your industry sector and potential regulatory requirements, you might need policies that address the physical security of all computing equipment, environmental security (protection against water, heat, or dust damage), and personnel security (protecting employees), just to name a few. Your cybersecurity insurance carrier might have additional requirements. Check with your cyber insurance carrier and possibly with the Information Sharing and Analysis Center (ISAC)[4] for your industry to see if they have policy templates or examples to meet their requirements. Keep in mind that policies simply dictate what can or cannot be done. To achieve the desired policy objectives, there are underlying technical security measures (hardware or software and configuration settings) that are used to implement the necessary controls.

- Create the following minimum set of policies, using the template from Appendix D.

    o User account management (identity and access management) [CIS Controls 16.8, 16.9, and 17.5]
    o Internet and email acceptable use [CIS Controls 7.1 and 7.7]

---

[4] Industry-specific Information Sharing and Analysis Centers (ISACs) collect and share timely security information and best practices. They constitute a public-private partnership with industry and law enforcement. See https://www.nationalisacs.org/ for more information.

- Protecting sensitive and confidential information [CIS Control 17.7]
- Virtual private network (VPN) and encryption [CIS Control 13.6]
- Wireless access and remote access [CIS Controls 15.7 and 15.10]
- Software updates and patch management [CIS Controls 3.4 and 3.5]
- Portable or mobile device security [CIS Control 13.6]
- System administration security [CIS Controls 4.3 and 6.2]
- Third-party access
- Identity theft awareness and training (FTC Red Flag Rule), if applicable

- After feedback from the "All Hands" meeting, make any necessary and agreed-upon changes to the policies, then implement them.

Step 4: Select a standard set of security controls to meet policy requirements

Rather than trying to "reinvent the wheel" and create your own control measures, you should use industry-standard security controls that will meet your business requirements. In addition, there are state and federal laws that require businesses to protect the personal information of their customers or clients. For example, in California the law (CA Civil Code §1798.81.5) states, "(b) A business that owns, licenses, or maintains personal information about a California resident shall implement and maintain reasonable security procedures and practices appropriate to the nature of the information, to protect the personal information from unauthorized access, destruction, use, modification, or disclosure." This law applies to any business with California customers, regardless of the state where the business is located. In 2016, the California Attorney General issued a report of cybercrimes and data breaches for 2011-2015. The first recommendation in this report informally defines what they consider "reasonable security." It states, "The 20 controls in the Center for Internet Security's Critical Security Controls define a minimum level of information security that all organizations that collect or maintain personal information should meet. The failure to implement all the Controls that apply to an organization's environment constitutes a lack of reasonable security." If your business operates or has customers in California, you should be aware of this "reasonableness" standard that the Attorney General's Office plans to use when investigating a breach. While not part of current law, this recommendation may impact a company's potential liability from an insurance or lawsuit perspective.

In April 2019, the CIS Controls® (or simply "Controls") were updated to version 7.1. They now include three Implementation Groups of Sub-Controls, which provide guidance for organizations of different sizes, technical complexity, and risk exposure. We recommend focusing on their Implementation Group 1 (IG1), which CIS considers to be "cyber hygiene" and provides selected Sub-Controls for small businesses with limited resources. We also recommend that small businesses perform a risk assessment to find any security gaps and determine the specific Sub-Controls needed to close those gaps. This includes the Sub-Controls in Implementation Groups 2 (IG2) and 3 (IG3) which would be applicable to their small business. Refer to Appendix B for links to the CIS Controls and Implementation Groups.

The primary CIS Controls are divided into three categories: Controls 1 through 6 are considered "basic," Controls 7 through 16 are "foundational," and Controls 17 through 20 are "organizational." Each of the primary Controls consist of several Sub-Controls, which provide more specific direction on implementing one specific security measure which, together, make up the larger control. Three implementation groups were created as a guide to help businesses of all sizes and industries determine what set of Sub-Controls might be appropriate for their specific needs and risk posture. The Sub-Controls within each Implementation Group are taken from across all of the Controls, based in part on the organization's level of technical complexity, the types of information assets being protected, the amount of internal or external resources the business has for cybersecurity, and the ease of implementing the Sub-Control. Table 9-1, below, lists the CIS Controls within their respective categories.

Basic	Foundational	Organizational
1. Inventory and Control of Hardware Assets	7. Email and Web Browser Protections	17. Implement a Security Training and Awareness Program
2. Inventory and Control of Software Assets	8. Malware Defenses	18. Application Software Security
3. Continuous Vulnerability Management	9. Limitation and Control of Network Ports, Protocols, and Services	19. Incident Response and Management
4. Controlled Use of Administrative Privileges	10. Data Recovery Capabilities	20. Penetration Tests and Red Team Exercises
5. Secure Configurations for Hardware and Software on Mobile Devices, Laptops, Workstations, and Servers	11. Secure Configurations for Network Devices, such as Firewalls, Routers, and Switches	
6. Maintenance, Monitoring, and Analysis of Audit Logs	12. Boundary Defense	
	13. Data Protection	
	14. Controlled Access Based on Need to Know	
	15. Wireless Access Control	
	16. Account Monitoring and Control	

Table 9-1. CIS Controls

IG1 contains the Sub-Controls listed in Table 9-2 below. The first column is used to indicate the level of technical skills needed to perform the task, with unshaded for non-technical (other than basic computer operation) and lightly shaded for having some experience with system configuration settings. There are no tasks which would indicate advanced skills are needed. In the first column there is also an indication of the potential cost for each Sub-Control. There will always be some minor cost for staff time to perform the task or for employee training, then increased costs when hardware or software are required. None of the Sub-Controls should require the hiring of a cybersecurity consultant unless you want that level of expertise to assist you.

CIS Controls® – Implementation Group 1	
Sub-Control # and Title	**Description**
$ 1.4 Maintain Detailed Asset Inventory	Maintain an accurate and up-to-date inventory of all technology assets with the potential to store or process information. This inventory shall include all assets, whether connected to the organization's network or not.
$ 1.6 Address Unauthorized Assets	Ensure that unauthorized assets are either removed from the network, quarantined or the inventory is updated in a timely manner.
$ 2.1 Maintain Inventory of Authorized Software	Maintain an up-to-date list of all authorized software that is required in the enterprise for any business purpose on any business system.
$ 2.2 Ensure Software is Supported by Vendor	Ensure that only software applications or operating systems currently supported and receiving vendor updates are added to the organization's authorized software inventory. Unsupported software should be tagged as unsupported in the inventory system.
$ 2.6 Address Unapproved Software	Ensure that unauthorized software is either removed or the inventory is updated in a timely manner.
$ 3.4 Deploy Automated Operating System Patch Management Tools	Deploy automated software update tools in order to ensure that the operating systems are running the most recent security updates provided by the software vendor.
$ 3.5 Deploy Automated Software Patch Management Tools	Deploy automated software update tools in order to ensure that third-party software on all systems is running the most recent security updates provided by the software vendor.
$ 4.2 Change Default Passwords	Before deploying any new asset, change all default passwords to have values consistent with administrative level accounts.
$ 4.3 Ensure the Use of Dedicated Administrative Accounts	Ensure that all users with administrative account access use a dedicated or secondary account for elevated activities. This account should only be used for administrative activities and not Internet browsing email or similar activities.

CIS Controls - Implementation Group 1	
Sub-Control # and Title	**Description**
$ 5.1 Establish Secure Configurations	Maintain documented security configuration standards for all authorized operating systems and software.
$ 6.2 Activate Audit Logging	Ensure that local logging has been enabled on all systems and networking devices.
$ 7.1 Ensure Use of Only Fully Supported Browsers and Email Clients	Ensure that only fully supported web browsers and email clients are allowed to execute in the organization, ideally only using the latest version of the browsers and email clients provided by the vendor.
$$ 7.7 Use of DNS Filtering Services	Use Domain Name System (DNS) filtering services to help block access to known malicious domains.
$ 8.2 Ensure Anti-Malware Software and Signatures are Updated	Ensure that the organization's anti-malware software updates its scanning engine and signature database on a regular basis.
$ 8.4 Configure Anti-Malware Scanning of Removable Media	Configure devices so that they automatically conduct an anti-malware scan of removable media when inserted or connected.
$ 8.5 Configure Devices to Not Auto-Run Content	Configure devices to not auto-run content from removable media.
$$ 9.4 Apply Host-Based Firewalls or Port-Filtering	Apply host-based firewalls or port-filtering tools on end systems, with a default-deny rule that drops all traffic except those services and ports that are explicitly allowed.
$ 10.1 Ensure Regular Automated Backups	Ensure that all system data is automatically backed up on a regular basis.
$ 10.2 Perform Complete System Backups	Ensure that all of the organization's key systems are backed up as a complete system, through processes such as imaging, to enable the quick recovery of an entire system.
$$ 10.4 Protect Backups	Ensure that backups are properly protected via physical security or encryption when they are stored, as well as when they are moved across the network. This includes remote backups and cloud services.
$$ 10.5 Ensure All Backups Have at least one Offline Backup Destination	Ensure that all backups have at least one offline (i.e., not accessible via a network connection) backup destination.
$ 11.4 Install the Latest Stable Version of any Security-Related Updates on All Network Devices	Install the latest stable version of any security related updates on all network devices.

CIS Controls® - Implementation Group 1		
	Sub-Control # and Title	**Description**
$	12.1 Maintain an Inventory of Network Boundaries	Maintain an up-to-date inventory of all of the organization's network boundaries.
$	12.4 Deny Communication Over Unauthorized Ports	Deny communication over unauthorized TCP or UDP ports or application traffic to ensure that only authorized protocols are allowed to cross the network boundary in or out of the network at each of the organization's network boundaries.
$	13.1 Maintain an Inventory of Sensitive Information	Maintain an inventory of all sensitive information stored, processed, or transmitted by the organization's technology systems, including those located on-site or at a remote service provider.
$	13.2 Remove Sensitive Data or Systems not Regularly Accessed by Organization	Remove sensitive data or systems not regularly accessed by the organization from the network These systems shall only be used as stand-alone systems (disconnected from the network) by the business unit needing to occasionally use the system or completely virtualized and powered off until needed.
$$	13.6 Encrypt Mobile Device Data	Utilize approved cryptographic mechanisms to protect enterprise data stored on all mobile devices.
$	14.6 Protect Information Through Access Control Lists (ACLs)	Protect all information stored on systems with file system, network share, claims, application or database specific access control lists. These controls will enforce the principle that only authorized individuals should have access to the information based on their need to access the information as a part of their responsibilities.
$$	15.7 Leverage the Advanced Encryption Standard (AES) to Encrypt Wireless Data	Leverage the Advanced Encryption Standard (AES) to encrypt wireless data in transit
$$	15.10 Create Separate Wireless Network for Personal and Untrusted Devices	Create a separate wireless network for personal or untrusted devices. Enterprise access from this network should be treated as untrusted and filtered and audited accordingly.
$	16.8 Disable any Unassociated Accounts	Disable any account that cannot be associated with a business process or business owner.
$	16.9 Disable Dormant Accounts	Automatically disable dormant accounts after a set period of inactivity.
$	16.11 Lock Workstation Sessions after Inactivity	Automatically lock workstation sessions after a standard period of inactivity.

CIS Controls® - Implementation Group 1		
	Sub-Control # and Title	Description
$$	17.3 Implement a Security Awareness Program	Create a security awareness program for all workforce members to complete on a regular basis to ensure they understand and exhibit the necessary behaviors and skills to help ensure the security of the organization. The organization's security awareness program should be communicated in a continuous and engaging manner.
$	17.5 Train Workforce on Secure Authentication	Train workforce members on the importance of enabling and utilizing secure authentication.
$	17.6 Train Workforce on Identifying Social Engineering Attacks	Train the workforce on how to identify different forms of social engineering attacks, such as phishing, phone scams, and impersonation calls.
$	17.7 Train Workforce on Sensitive Data Handling	Train workforce members on how to identify and properly store, transfer, archive, and destroy sensitive information.
$	17.8 Train Workforce on Causes of Unintentional Data Exposure	Train workforce members to be aware of causes for unintentional data exposures, such as losing their mobile devices or emailing the wrong person due to autocomplete in email.
$	17.9 Train Workforce Members on Identifying and Reporting Incidents	Train workforce members to be able to identify the most common indicators of an incident and be able to report such an incident.
$	19.1 Document Incident Response Procedures	Ensure that there are written incident response plans that define roles of personnel as well as phases of incident handling/management.
$	19.3 Designate Management Personnel to Support Incident Handling	Designate management personnel, as well as backups, who will support the incident handling process by acting in key decision-making roles.
$	19.5 Maintain Contact Information for Reporting Security Incidents	Assemble and maintain information on third party contact information to be used to report a security incident, such as Law Enforcement, relevant government departments, vendors, and Information Sharing and Analysis Center (ISAC) partners.
$	19.6 Publish Information Regarding Computer Anomalies and Incidents	Publish information for all workforce members, regarding reporting computer anomalies and incidents to the incident handling team. Such information should be included in routine employee awareness activities.

You should rank the 43 Sub-Controls in IG1 from most to least appropriate and applicable to your small business. Then, determine the order in which you will implement the Sub-Controls; for example, starting with the no-cost, non-technical ones, or starting with the ones you believe will have the greatest risk-reduction benefit. Several of the Sub-Control tasks are meant to be combined through the use of automation, especially for hardware and software inventory management. Configuration management is similar, although different enough to warrant a separate automated system, which in most cases can be integrated with a vulnerability assessment system.

As one example, implementing a few basic monitoring systems to automate inventory discovery and tracking can cause us to address what happens when unauthorized hardware or software is discovered. These no-cost tasks should be addressed in the security policies, so that the unauthorized (unapproved) device or software is either removed and denied access or added to the authorized list of hardware or software via an approval process.

Now that you have decided which Sub-Controls to implement, in a prioritized sequence, this is a good point at which to align performance measures and success factors with each one. Luckily, CIS has a full set of "Measures and Metrics for CIS Controls v7," so you don't have to create them from scratch (refer to the resource link in Appendix B). Let's look at one IG1 Sub-Control as an example:

Sub-Control 4.3 – Ensure the use of dedicated administrative accounts

Control Objective: Ensure that all users with administrative account access use a dedicated or secondary account for elevated activities. This account should only be used for administrative activities and not internet browsing, email, or similar activities (which should be done using their standard user account).

<u>Measure</u>: What percentage of the organization's user accounts with elevated rights do <u>not</u> utilize a dedicated or secondary account for elevated activities?

Goal: 4% or less (this is something you will determine for each measure)

<u>Results</u>:   Excellent = 6% or less
                 Good = 10% or less
                 Acceptable = 15% or less
                 Poor = 20% or less
                 Unacceptable = 25% or less

If your organization only has two people performing these elevated activities, then ideally both of them would be complying with the control measure. However, the percentages given for each result level would be irrelevant because as soon as one of the two people violate the rule, the result becomes 50% (unacceptable). You should choose metrics that will be meaningful to your business and set the goals for those metrics to meet your business expectations.

While the CIS Measures and Metrics document only provides one primary measure for each Sub-Control, you may create your own internal measures and goals to be achieved for any particular Sub-Control. There is also an online CIS community of practitioners who may offer additional measures and metrics used in other organizations around the world.

Chapter 9 – Recommended Action Items

- Adopt the applicable Sub-Controls from the CIS Controls IG1, following the category groupings of similar Sub-Controls as listed in Section 5, such as those related to asset management. Implementation is addressed in Step 7 in Chapter 10, with details in Section 5.

- Discuss the use of the Sub-Controls with your employees so that they know the purpose behind each control measure, how the controls potentially relate to their job functions, and the importance of everyone being responsible for working within any constraints created by the Sub-Controls. Stress the fact that the control measures protect the company's ability to operate safely and reduce overall business risks. This is a pre-implementation step, not part of a cybersecurity awareness program.

- Create a mechanism for employees to provide feedback about any Sub-Controls that are negatively impacting their job functions. In many cases it will be a matter of properly training employees to work within the security limitations, while at other times it may just require fine-tuning some configuration settings.

Chapter 10

Building Your Cybersecurity Plan and Selecting Your Controls

Now we'll continue further down the path of implementing your cybersecurity program and preparing to respond to external events. We will cover the following six steps in this chapter; the first four steps will complete the governance document we started in Chapter 9, and the final two steps will begin implementation of the program.

- Step 5 – Create and implement a cybersecurity awareness and training program
- Step 6 – Incorporate cybersecurity into the business emergency management plan
- Step 7 – Create and implement a cybersecurity incident response plan
- Step 8 – Set up regular reviews of the cybersecurity program for the first year and on an ongoing basis
- Step 9 – Develop a schedule for phased implementation of security controls
- Step 10 – Conduct an "All Hands" orientation on the cybersecurity program

Step 5: Create and implement a cybersecurity awareness and training program

One of the key factors for having a successful cybersecurity program is ensuring that the organization's employees and trusted business partners understand the cybersecurity policies and procedures through a formalized awareness and training program. As you might deduce from the title, this is actually a two-part program – the "training" component is a more formalized, structured set of sessions where employees are given necessary briefings on the organization's security policies and procedures. The "awareness" component is more fluid and provides periodic and ongoing reminders about safe computing practices. Human Resources will want to verify that each employee has completed the required training sessions, as well as the annual review and any periodic update sessions. Usually, employees will sign an acknowledgment that they have completed the training, that they understand the policies and procedures, and that they agree to comply with them. Some organizations keep the training verification separate from the employee acknowledgment of understanding and compliance. Employees should be notified in advance of the expectations to attend training, and it is a good business practice to include this information in a "new hire" package.

The awareness part of this program is intended to provide simple, one-topic prompts to help build a cybersecurity mindset into the company's work culture. The awareness materials should be fun and interesting, and should come in various formats, for example any combination of these:

- Visual – posters, electric signs, screen saver messages, desktop notes, etc.
- Audio – a short recorded message that plays when the user logs in, or a recorded message that plays periodically in a lunch/break room
- Audio-video – short video clips that automatically play on user workstations during the day, a video message that plays on a monitor in a lunch/break room, or a video message that plays during staff meetings
- Live sessions – informal, brown-bag lunch information session with IT and security staff
- Live webcast with Q&A time (recorded for those who are not able to participate)

- Specific, informal discussion sessions for particular workgroups/teams

These are all just examples of some activities and methods of providing cybersecurity awareness for the organization. Almost all of them can be no-cost or very low-cost, and the potential benefits for having "cyber-aware" employees should exceed any costs.

- Create an overall description of the awareness and training program by completing section 4.4 of the strategy document.
- Using the separate template in Appendix D, create your cybersecurity awareness and training program. [CIS Controls 17.3, 17.5, 17.6, 17.7, 17.8, and 17.9]
- Refer to Step 10 below for information on holding an "All Hands" meeting to introduce the new cybersecurity program components.
- After the initial orientation sessions, schedule regular training sessions and hold informal awareness activities periodically over the next year.

Step 6: Incorporate cybersecurity into the business emergency management plan

Using an "All Hazards" perspective for emergency management planning, you should include known cyber risks along with other natural or man-made disasters. The risks and respective actions to be taken should be part of the Business Continuity Plan (BCP) and Disaster Recovery Plan (DRP).

- Using the basic information provided in the strategy template in Appendix D, and the results from any risk assessments you have performed, add the identified cyber risks into your BCP and DRP documents.
- For BCP purposes, you should have determined which systems are considered critical for keeping your business

operational, and how much downtime can occur before negative impacts start to affect the business.

- If the emergency involves physical danger, then the first priority is always the safety of your employees and anyone in your offices, so both the BCP and DRP should describe necessary procedures to protect human life, such as escape routes or sheltering in place, depending on the circumstances.

- For each critical asset (computer systems or data), you should outline what needs to happen to bring it back into basic operation (for BCP) or potentially to restore systems at an alternate site or wherever your procedures dictate (for DRP).

- Keep in mind that computer failures may occur as a result of natural or man-made disasters, not directly related to a cyberattack. Be prepared to address combinations of physical impacts (flooding, fires, earthquakes, tornados, etc.) and related computer system impacts. Cyberattacks fall into the category of man-made disasters.

- Prior to restoring computer system operations, you will need to ensure that basic utilities are functioning, for example, that your office building has emergency power generators and multiple Internet connections.

- Your plans should include the contact information for your ISP or CSP because they will have their own emergency procedures, and you will need to know how those affect your services and what they will commit to doing to restore your services.

Step 7. Create and implement a cybersecurity incident response plan

Unlike the BCP and DRP, which address the aftermath of a cyberattack, this incident response plan addresses what happens during (response) and immediately following an attack (recovery).

- Within the strategy document, you only need to define the cybersecurity incident response plan, including designation of a position to oversee the incident response process. You do not need to include details in the strategy document. Use the separate template in Appendix D to create the actual incident response plan.

- Depending on the size of your business and the resources you have available for handling cyber incidents, your incident response plan can be as simple as a checklist or it can be a more comprehensive plan and policy. Both types of templates can be found in Appendix D.

- If you are going to use the simple checklist template, then you should go back to the strategy document and include some more details about roles and responsibilities for incident response. This way, the scope and nature of tasks to be performed are clear, such as who is responsible for each item on the checklist.

- If you are going to use the larger response plan template, the first key task is to identify roles and responsibilities, removing any that are not applicable to your small business. Then, customize the rest of the template to create a plan that fits your requirements and resources.

Step 8. Set up regular reviews of the cybersecurity program for the first year and on an ongoing basis

There are two major parts to this step. First, plan periodic (quarterly) reviews of the cybersecurity program over the first year of implementation. As with any major business initiative, you will want to incorporate metrics for measuring the success of implementing a cybersecurity program. At the end of this part of Step 8, you should be conducting an evaluation of the success of the implementation "project." The purpose of this part of the step is to measure how well the cybersecurity program is working up through the first year. In the second part of Step 8, we will discuss the process of ongoing measurement of the program and seeking continuous improvement.

- Evaluate the security program implementation, separate from evaluating the phased implementation "project." The following list provides some general measures that may apply to your business; however, there might be additional metrics that you want to include, based on your specific situation (i.e., for regulatory compliance or insurance requirements). Note that the term "employees" as used below includes the owner, CEO, President (and other officers), and all levels from executive management to entry-level workers.

- For each quarter of the first year during and after implementation, take these point-in-time measurements that indicate how well performance goals are being met:

  o How many employees completed the mandatory security policy training?
  o Have all the critical information assets been identified? How complete is the asset inventory (hardware and software)?
  o How many unauthorized hardware devices or software programs have been identified and resolved?
  o How many security awareness sessions were held, or how many security awareness posters or other resources were displayed or distributed?

- For each quarter of the first year during and after implementation, take these cumulative measurements that should show a progression toward increased security:

  o How many potential security incidents have been reported by employees?
  o How many potential intrusion attempts were detected and blocked by new security control measures? (You should note that this metric can vary widely, based on many factors, and could range from 100 to 1,000,000. It

may be more beneficial to know how many intrusion attempts were successful in bypassing new security measures.)

o   If applicable, how many attempts to access malicious or inappropriate websites were blocked by a web filtering system?

o   If applicable, how many potential phishing or other malicious email messages were captured or blocked and never reached employee email inboxes? If any potential phishing messages did get through to employee email inboxes, how many employees clicked on a malicious link?

o   After the first year, has the number of security policy violations increased, decreased, or stayed the same?

- Select from the list of example questions above or create your own evaluation questions to judge the success of implementing your cybersecurity program, including specific Sub-Controls. These questions and metrics should relate to how well the program security measures are functioning, and not to how well implementation goals were met.

- Start a quarterly review of the cybersecurity program during implementation, rather than simply using project milestones. This should create standard timing for continuing on an ongoing basis after the first year.

- Review the results from the evaluation questions and take appropriate action to make corrections to control measures or modify procedures. Be aware of those measures which will not have a satisfactory result until after the full implementation effort has been completed. In those cases, there should be a progression toward attaining measurement goals with each quarterly review.

- Keep track of the progress and measurements from each quarterly review for comparison with the overall, end-of-implementation review and with the first annual review in the following year.

The second major part of Step 8 is to set up an ongoing, annual review and update process for the cybersecurity program. This basically implements the cybersecurity program lifecycle, as opposed to the cybersecurity functions lifecycle. If you recall from Chapter 6, the initial program lifecycle consists of the phases the table 10-1.

Phase	Implementation Lifecycle
1	Define/Refine Requirements
2	Develop & Initiate Strategy
3	Create Policies & Identify Controls
4	Implement Policies & Controls
5	Evaluate Implementation Effectiveness

Table 10-1. Implementation Lifecycle by Phase

Basically, the focus changes from creating and implementing new policies, procedures, and business practices, to reviewing, evaluating, fine-tuning, and updating them. The long-term strategies may be reviewed annually, then changed or updated every three to five years. Business goals and objectives related to cybersecurity may change when needed, such as when the business launches a new line of products or services, or new regulatory requirements are issued. For the annual review cycle, there is not necessarily a specific set of metrics to be calculated and evaluated; it is a more subjective analysis. However, evaluating the effectiveness of the overall program should be as objective as possible. Now the ongoing lifecycle phases are introduced table 10-2.

Phase	Ongoing Lifecycle
1	Review/Update Requirements
2	Review/Update Strategy & Objectives
3	Review/Update Policies & Controls
4	Test Policies & Controls
5	Evaluate Program Effectiveness

Table 10-2. Ongoing Lifecycle by Phase

One new step in the annual review cycle is testing the policies and controls. This can be done through vulnerability assessments, followed by penetration testing. It can also include drills and exercises, to observe how your staff and any outside parties (e.g., ISP or CSP) respond to a simulated cyberattack. Testing the policies and procedures among staff may involve their participation in simulations or taking a quiz. The purpose behind the testing is to determine the current level of effectiveness and whether there are gaps between what the policy states and what is actually happening. Some of the tests may not be practical or affordable for your small business, in which case you would perform only those tests and evaluations that can be done within your resources and level of expertise.

- Follow the direction from your cybersecurity strategy and program description, where you defined an ongoing, annual review process. Select dates on the calendar for conducting the first review, approximately one year after implementation is complete.

- o You may want to have this review coincide with other annual business processes. If doing so results in a review period that is less than six months following completion of the implementation of the cybersecurity program, you may want to delay the initial review until 18 months have passed.

- Evaluate the major components of the cybersecurity program – (1) achieving strategic goals and objectives, (2) achieving employee training goals, (3) effectiveness of security control measures, and (4) compliance with cybersecurity policies. Use standardized metrics, if possible, such as the CIS Measures and Metrics for each Sub-Control (as discussed in Step 4 in Chapter 9).

  - o If you have regulatory compliance or insurance carrier requirements, ensure that you are monitoring and capturing the correct security data to meet their reporting requirements.

- If you rely on your ISP or CSP (or other third-party contracts) for some of the security requirements, be sure they are aware of your annual review cycle and especially what data you require from them and when it is due.

  - o Performance and other types of service metrics should be part of the company's contract with the ISP or CSP, including regular reporting (usually monthly).

- After completing the reviews of the different cybersecurity program components, and analyzing the results, the executive management team reviews them and decides if changes need to be made. Changes may apply to the overall cybersecurity program, the strategy, or any policies and procedures, to improve cybersecurity, decrease risk, and enhance effectiveness. The cycle continues with the implementation and monitoring of any changes and evaluating the new level of effectiveness after three months and six months, with the focus on continuous improvement.

o   Another metric is to ensure that all employees attend a refresher training session on the policies and procedures, with emphasis on any changes made.

Step 9: Develop a schedule for phased implementation of security controls

After creating your prioritized list of Sub-Controls to be implemented (from Step 4 in Chapter 9), you should create an implementation schedule. To better ensure success, I encourage you to run the implementation as a project. A project will create roles and responsibilities for each task, along with an acceptable timeline. Even if you don't create an actual project, the person responsible for implementation should view it and manage it as a project. Planning the schedule should include members of each business unit that will be impacted by each phase (which may be the whole organization for a small business).

- The phased implementation schedule should take the following factors into account:
- The availability of staff who will be performing the implementation tasks
- Regular business operations, so as to cause the least amount of disruption
- The number of devices (workstations, laptops, servers, routers, etc.) that will need to be configured or updated
- The Sub-Controls that can be implemented concurrently as parallel tasks
- The number of phases expected (how many iterations to complete implementation?); for example, if you plan to

implement controls for 25% of your staff in each phase, there will be four phases.

- A contingency plan to revert back to prior operational modes, in case something fails during implementation

There are two primary methods to schedule the implementation of security controls – task-oriented and workgroup-oriented. The task-oriented method uses the project phases to implement small sets of Sub-Controls across the whole organization. The workgroup-oriented method uses each phase to implement the full set of Sub-Controls for designated workgroups in each phase. A small business should probably use the task-oriented method because of the relatively small number of people. Plan the tasks and activities for each phase to last for one week, using the weekends as a natural divider between phases. During the time between phases, testing of newly implemented Sub-Controls can occur. If this schedule is too aggressive for your organization, then extend either the phase timeline (perhaps to two weeks) or the testing period (possibly to one full week), or both if needed. It's important to get the security measures implemented correctly and not to rush to get them completed. Doing it right the first time avoids having to go back to make corrections, which would result in higher costs from the time and effort to fix what was not done properly.

As a small business, let's assume you are going to use the task-oriented method. Looking back at the 43 Sub-Controls in IG1, Table 9-2 under Step 4 identifies 11 Sub-Controls that are somewhat technical; the remaining 32 Sub-Controls are basically non-technical. Let's assume it takes three weeks to put the first 32 non-technical Sub-Controls in place (ten per week). Then assume it takes two weeks to put the remaining 11 Sub-Controls in place (five per week). This results in five phases of implementation, and you will also need to include time for testing and fixing any problems between each phase. If you allow one week between phases, your planned implementation will occur over ten weeks. In addition, at the conclusion of testing for the final scheduled phase, there should be a time period (e.g., two weeks) for a final evaluation of the overall success of the implementation project before it is considered complete. Under these assumptions, the full implementation process would take three months, which may be a rather aggressive schedule for some businesses. Therefore, you will need to plan the schedule to match your resources and operations.

During implementation, there are several potential metrics that can be used to measure both the status of the project and the success of implementing the program. Project metrics should be simple – is it on schedule, have the milestones been met, and is it within budget? Variations in schedule and cost may be acceptable to management if they are justified with legitimate business reasons. For example, a delay in implementing an automated inventory management system caused by the vendor not delivering on time due to a fire at their warehouse. Another example would be an unplanned, critical business requirement (such as a surge in customer requests that exceeds normal production), which cannot be interrupted to implement certain security controls, causes a one-week delay.

- Refer to Section 5 for recommendations on starting to implement categories of the Sub-Controls, which are grouped by a common purpose, and to gain some understanding of the potential scope and resource requirements. You may consider using the described categories as the separation of phases.
- Select someone for the role of project manager to be in charge of the implementation effort. This should be someone who can coordinate schedules with executives and employees and keep the implementation on time and within budget. This person does not necessarily need to be the one with technical expertise related to the Sub-Controls.
- Identify the person or persons who will be performing the implementation tasks. This will require having at least some

expertise for implementing the few Sub-Controls that are more technical.

- Create your own phased implementation schedule based on the factors discussed above and your own business circumstances.

- Perform limited evaluations at the end of each phase or milestone completion to validate the successful implementation of applicable Sub-Controls for that time period.

  o Success may be defined as having the Sub-Controls in place, active, and functioning as expected, with minimal or no impact on business operations. (Some minimal impact is to be expected, as is the case with implementing any new work procedures.)

  o What percentage of (and how many) security controls were implemented and became operational during the review period? How does this compare with the implementation plan?

- Conduct an end-of-implementation evaluation and review upon completing the implementation of all applicable Sub-Controls.

Step 10: Conduct an "All Hands" orientation for employees on the cybersecurity program (especially the policies)

This should be done when creating a new cybersecurity program, whether your business has been in operation for some time or is a start-up. This should be a simple and mostly informal meeting, especially for a small business, and should not be a surprise to anyone. This means that advance notice along with copies of pertinent documents should be provided to all employees, with instructions to provide any questions in advance to a designated person (such as the

Owner, CEO/President or CISO) at least a few days prior to the meeting so that answers can be prepared.

- As you are completing the necessary documents (strategy, program definition, policies, and procedures) and obtaining employee feedback during that process, you should plan for an open-forum type of meeting with all employees to discuss the cybersecurity program being created. This is often called an "All Hands" meeting, a term derived from sailing or the Navy, where it's "all hands, on deck."

- Even though we use the term "All Hands" meeting, this does not mean that the organization needs to halt all of its operations for every employee to attend this meeting. We expect all employees to receive the same in-person briefing, but larger organizations will usually hold departmental meetings or in groups by office location.

- The purpose of this "All Hands" meeting is to provide the employees with an overview of the cybersecurity program, and with an understanding that this is something executive management is supporting and implementing.

- This should be an informal meeting focused on information sharing. Allow at least 90 minutes for the meeting.

- A designated executive should facilitate the meeting, for example, the CEO, President, CIO, CFO, or the VP over each department where the meeting is being held. Present the background information about why a cybersecurity program is needed and how it will help the organization reduce overall risk. Explain that every employee plays a part in keeping the organizations' information assets safe and secure. Provide an overview of each of the program documents and inform employees that there will be more formalized training on the policies and procedures.

- As you advertise the meeting, link the need for the cybersecurity program to the pervasive use of technology in businesses, and emphasize that the cybersecurity program is intended to provide guidance to employees on safe computing practices. This in turn leads to decreased chances of becoming the victim of a cyber-attack, which reduces overall business risk levels, and benefits the whole company. Make it personal.

- This meeting is a chance to get buy-in from employees on the different components of the program, especially the policies and procedures which will directly affect them. Be sure to explain the reasoning behind each policy or procedure, so the employees can better understand WHY certain rules are being implemented and WHAT they are trying to accomplish. Demonstrate, as much as possible, how the various policies and procedures enable business functions to operate securely, in order to protect the company's confidential information and your customer's data.

- It may be helpful to create a FAQ (frequently asked questions) sheet that contains both questions and answers, which is available to all employees. This can be posted on an internal employee intranet page or printed and posted on a bulletin board or use some other means of internal distribution.

Now that you have taken steps to create, define, and implement your cybersecurity program, we will look at how to begin implementing some of the actual Sub-Controls in Section 5.

Executing Your Cybersecurity Plan

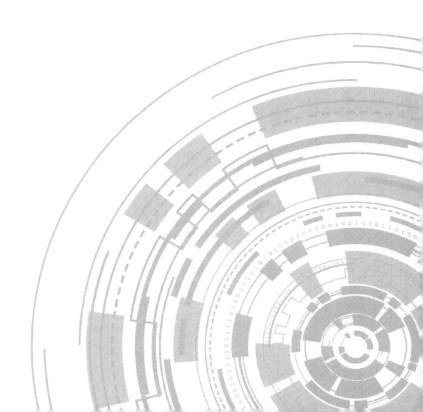

> *"I often describe the CIS Critical Security Controls as a 'security best practices framework.' A useful security framework is much more than a list or an end goal. A useful security framework is like a 'machine' or process that helps you gather information, make reasonable choices, and develop and execute a plan of positive, constructive action – and then be able to explain to others what you are doing, and where you are on the journey."*
>
> *Tony Sager, Executive Vice President & Controls Evangelist, CIS*

Congratulations – you made it through all of the background materials and the steps to create your own cybersecurity program. In this section, you will learn the beginning steps for setting up some basic security measures considered by CIS to comprise good cyber hygiene. The purpose of this section is to get your small business protected at a minimum level so you can build from there. By creating a cybersecurity program, with its related policies and procedures, along with a training and awareness program, you are already achieving several control objectives.

Two key points which should lead to long-term success for your program are worth repeating:

1. IT and cybersecurity should be enablers of, not hindrances to, your business processes and operations. It usually takes an effort to keep them that way. Business innovation and flexibility can actually improve within a secure computing environment. It depends upon everyone remembering the

purpose for the security measures and not trying to undermine or bypass them. We put brakes on cars so we can go fast, not to go slow.

2. A good cybersecurity awareness program will go a long way toward having employees incorporate safe computing habits into their daily work duties and creating a cybersecure work culture. Rather than focusing on the negative consequences of violating policies, the awareness program is meant to encourage and reward employees for doing the right things to protect the company's information assets, including customer information.

How This Section Is Organized

From Chapter 9, you should have created a prioritized list of the IG1 Sub-Controls that you plan to implement for your small business. This section will explain how to implement most of those Sub-Controls from a non-technical perspective. We will categorize all 43 of the Sub-Controls in IG1 and then separate out those Sub-Controls that you can implement in your small business with little effort. Chapter 12 will start with a checklist of some of the very basic Sub-Controls from IG1 that will create the foundation for continuing to build upon the security infrastructure and control measures. Then, Chapters 13-15 contain detailed instructions for implementing most of the IG1 Sub-Controls (37 out of the 43). Even though the instructions are as non-technical as possible, many of these controls will require some basic or intermediate level of knowledge or experience with various computer systems.

For the most part, the Sub-Controls here will be presented in numeric order within each category and will likely be different from the sequence of your priority list. You do not need to follow the sequence presented here. As a matter of fact, you can simply use your own sequence and find the implementation instructions in this section for a particular Sub-Control. However, we strongly recommend that you take care of the asset inventory items first

(Group 1, Sub-Controls 1.4, 1.6, 2.1, 2.2, and 2.6), because if you don't know what you are trying to protect and where it is located, you won't be able to select proper security measures.

Categorizing Security Controls within IG1

In Chapters 13-15, we've grouped interrelated Sub-Controls into categories to facilitate implementation, especially where the same software tools can be applied across two or more Sub-Controls. For the purpose of implementing related groups of the CIS Sub-Controls from IG1, the following groupings will be used (with the relevant Sub-Controls listed). While all 43 Sub-Controls have been assigned to a category below, not all Sub-Controls within each category will have implementation instructions in this book. We will cover 37 out of the 43 Sub-Controls in Chapters 13-15.

The Sub-Controls are organized so that in Chapter 13 you are hardening the infrastructure. Handling this first provides a good foundation for your security. Next, you address your user base, addressing user security controls and awareness so you have a cyber-aware workforce operating within the confines of your Sub-Controls. With these two essential "layers" of security in place, you can move on to securing sensitive data and preparing for the incidents that might jeopardize your operations or expose sensitive data.

Group 1 (Chapter 12) – Administrative and Configuration Controls

Asset Management (hardware and software)
Sub-Controls: 1.4, 1.6, 2.1, 2.2, and 2.6

Basic System Administration
Sub-Controls: 3.4, 3.5, 6.2, 8.2, 9.4, 10.1, 10.2, 10.4, 10.5,
                  11.4, 14.6, and 16.11

Configuration Management
Sub-Controls: 5.1, 7.1, 7.7, 8.4, 8.5, 12.1, 12.4, 15.7, and
                  15.10

Group 2 (Chapter 13) – User Controls and Training

User Administration
Sub-Controls: 4.2, 4.3, 16.8, and 16.9

Cybersecurity Awareness and Training
Sub-Controls: 17.3, 17.5, 17.6, 17.7, 17.8, and 17.9

Group 3 (Chapter 14) – Incident and Breach Controls

Protecting Sensitive or Confidential Information
Sub-Controls: 13.1, 13.2, and 13.6

Incident Response Management
Sub-Controls: 19.1, 19.3, 19.5, and 19.6

Please note that the mention of a particular product or service to help implement the CIS Sub-Controls is strictly for illustrative purposes, as an example for potential implementation, and is solely that of the author; it does not imply or constitute a direct or indirect endorsement of the products or services by CIS or CISO DRG, Inc..

Chapter 11

The Key CIS Sub-Controls for Small Businesses

Now comes the hard work – putting into practice the security policies and procedures you have created. This chapter will help you implement simple control measures that are primarily procedural and take little if any technical knowledge or expertise. Before starting, the following assumptions have been made in creating these instructions. Slight variations from these assumptions may not have an impact on successful implementation; however, moderate to major variations will possibly render the controls ineffective.

- Your business uses a combination of applications, where some are installed and running on local computers and some are hosted by a cloud service
- You have the contact information for support from your ISP or CSP, who in accordance with your service contract will provide necessary services for setting up security measures within their areas of responsibility

Remember, the CSP is responsible for maintaining and updating the online infrastructure and operating environment (in other words, they keep their physical and virtual machines up to date with security patches), as well as maintaining their application software.

Illustrative commands are provided throughout these final few chapters to give a sense of the keystrokes needed to complete the tasks. Rather than hop back and forth between the three major computing platforms that are likely in use (Microsoft® Windows®, Linux and, Mac OS®), I've chosen to demonstrate only with the Windows version (specifically compatible with version 8.1 or 10 Professional [Win-8 Pro or Win-10 Pro]). Please see Appendix B for resources where you might find applicable tutorials for other computing platforms.

Implementing the Bare Bones Controls

As mentioned, you should start with your asset inventory, both hardware and software. While it is best to have a software tool that automates the collection and management of your asset inventory, you can start by using a spreadsheet. Use the template in Appendix D for the physical inventory data collection. Then cross-reference what you find with your purchase records (if available). When using the template, create and save a file for each asset, filling in as much of the inventory information as possible for each one. [Sub-Controls 1.4 and 2.1]

While performing the physical inventory, there are some steps you can take to help prepare for using an automated tool at a later time. As you gather the information from each device, you will need to be logged in to get certain details. Take a few moments to ensure the following:

- Each workstation, laptop, tablet or other computing device that allows a user to log in should be configured to accept and validate individual User IDs separately instead of having a single Administrator account login
- Include Virtual Machines (VMs) that are created and used on a regular basis as part of the physical inventory, if applicable
- Only one or two authorized employees should have access to the login credentials for the Local Administrator account(s), which should be the same for all end-user devices
- Only one or two authorized employees should have access to the login credentials for Administrator account(s) on network devices and servers

Ensure that the following settings are configured by using the system administrative settings, either locally on each individual device or from a centrally managed console (for example, Active Directory or a similar, centralized management tool):

- Windows Update is enabled to automatically download and install "critical" and "important" updates (patches), including other Microsoft products, only for non-critical business systems [Sub-Control 3.4]

  - Security patches/updates for critical business systems should be tested on the non-critical systems before installation on critical business systems

- Windows Firewall is enabled on all workstations, laptops, tablets, or other devices running Windows OS, with the default settings to block all traffic except for applications, services, or ports that are explicitly allowed [Sub-Control 9.4]

- Select, install, and enable anti-malware software – you can use Windows Defender or another package of your choice (such as McAfee, Norton/Symantec, Bitdefender, ESET, Kaspersky, or Webroot, which all have appropriate packages for small businesses)

  - Enable real-time scanning, as well as scheduled "quick scans" every time the system is turned on and boots up

  - Enable scanning of any portable or removable device any time one is connected to the computer or data is accessed from or saved to the device (NOTE – *Windows Defender* cannot perform an automated scan when files are accessed or saved on removable media; for that, you would need to use a different commercial package) [Sub-Control 8.4]

  - Enable scanning of email messages and attachments; if available, enable SPAM protection

- o Enable automatic updates of the malware signature files and security patches for the anti-malware software [Sub-Control 8.2]
- o Enable and schedule full system scans to occur weekly

- Check for user login accounts that are not assigned to a unique individual (person) and disable them [Sub-Control 16.8]
- Check for user login accounts that have been inactive (dormant) beyond the limit set in your cybersecurity policy and disable them [Sub-Control 16.9]
- Set the screen saver for all workstations, laptops, and tablets to be enabled after fifteen (15) minutes of inactivity and require login credentials to clear the screen saver and return to normal operations [Sub-Control 16.11]
- For any new device, especially network devices (such as wired or wireless routers, firewalls, and gateways), be sure to change the default password to something that is unique and follows the requirements of your password policy [Sub-Control 4.2]

For each device (workstation or server) where you store or maintain your business data and documents, set up automatic, incremental backups to occur daily. [Sub-Control 10.1] This saves any files or data that were changed since the last backup. You should also configure a full system backup to run automatically on at least a monthly basis, preferably weekly. [Sub-Control 10.2] The backup data may be saved to a cloud storage location or to an external hard drive attached to the device. If your data is stored in a cloud service, coordinate with your CSP on setting up regular backups and have them provide you with a copy on a weekly or bi-weekly basis. Ideally, you should have multiple external hard drives that can be rotated each week to use as the backup storage location. The detached drives should be stored in a locked, fire-proof cabinet to protect against theft or damage. [Sub-Control 10.5]

Separately from all of the system configuration settings, take steps to implement your cybersecurity awareness and training program.

- Have management approve and adopt the cybersecurity strategic plan, along with the accompanying cybersecurity program documents, including policies and procedures [Sub-Control 17.3]
- Conduct employee training sessions for the cybersecurity policies and procedures, specifically covering these five topics, among others:
  - o Secure authentication [Sub-Control 17.5]
  - o Identifying social engineering attacks [Sub-Control 17.6]
  - o Sensitive information handling [Sub-Control 17.7]
  - o Causes of unintentional data exposure [Sub-Control 17.8]
  - o Identifying and reporting cybersecurity incidents [Sub-Control 17.9]
- Initiate an employee awareness campaign

As part of the approved cybersecurity policies and procedures, ensure that you have a procedure in place to take care of unauthorized hardware or software that is found during the inventory – either to have the unauthorized item removed or to have it added to the official inventory. [Sub-Controls 1.6 and 2.6]

Finally, as a component of your cybersecurity incident response plan and procedures:

- Maintain an updated list of contacts (name, phone number, and email address) for your ISP or CSP; specifically, those contacts responsible for incident response, not just customer service [Sub-Control 19.5]
- Maintain an updated list of other contacts related to incident response, including third-party contractors (if applicable), local law enforcement, FBI Cyber Crime Squad, any

regulatory agency for your industry (if applicable), other government agencies that may provide support (i.e., SBA or FTC), your cybersecurity insurance carrier, and any vendors who may provide their support [Sub-Control 19.5]

- Optional, but recommended, is to also maintain a contact list of key customers whom you want to notify regarding any disruption of services; this is to help maintain the customers' trust, not for them to assist with incident response
- Ensure that all your employees are aware of how to recognize a potential cyberattack, plus how, when, and where to report a potential cybersecurity incident [Sub-Control 19.6]

Chapter 12

Implementing Administrative and Configuration Controls

Now that you have created a basic foundation for cybersecurity through your governance program and implementing some of the key Sub-Controls in Chapter 11, we can continue with more detailed instructions. You will find duplication of some Sub-Controls in this section because we will be automating several tasks that were implemented manually in the previous chapter. As before, we have used the Windows OS in our examples; there are similar features available in macOS and Linux.

In those instances where multiple Sub-Controls can be achieved using a common method (whether automated through software or in a manual process), those Sub-Controls will be grouped together. Otherwise, there will be instructions for individual Sub-Controls. As with Chapter 11, here are some basic assumptions we have made for Chapters 12, 13, and 14:

- Internal to your business or through contract services, the person performing the implementation:

    o has basic computer skills for viewing and setting system configuration parameters on workstations, laptops, and notebooks (refer to Appendix B for some helpful tutorial videos)

    o has the appropriate, system-level administrative access rights to all devices that need to be set up or configured

    o knows how to view and configure network settings on workstations, laptops, and notebooks

- o knows how to modify and configure system and network security settings, including how to manage user access rights by using security groups
- o knows how to configure basic settings on a network or local firewall
- o knows how to configure basic settings on a wireless access point (router), including the creation of both trusted network access for authorized devices and a separate guest network for untrusted devices

- A person with a more advanced level of technical experience also understands the basics of Microsoft's Active Directory and how to manage and configure a domain controller, including defining a forest and domains and using Group Policy Objects (GPOs)

Implementing IG1 Sub-Controls for Asset Management (5 of 5 Sub-Controls)

Implementing Sub-Controls 1.4 (Maintain a detailed asset inventory) and 2.1 (Maintain an inventory of authorized software)

These Sub-Controls can be implemented together, using a single asset management software solution. There are several free and reasonably priced commercial packages available with varying degrees of complexity and functionality that can be used locally within an office network or through a cloud-based service. Whichever package you use, follow the prompts during the installation to enter some basic information about your assets. You will also be prompted to enter administrative-level user credentials, which gives the software access to your devices.

To prepare for managing your assets and before running an automated tool, regardless of which one you choose, follow the recommended preparatory actions from Chapter 12, and these additional steps that will make the automated process work more smoothly:

- Special case systems must be configured to allow automated scanning with the Administrator credentials, but not allow direct login. In other words, the asset management software is allowed to run using its designated credentials, but a person cannot use the same credentials to login to the device.
- Most employees should not be given access to the asset management system; it should be restricted to authorized employees who are responsible for IT assets and technical support.
  Some automated tools can set up a user portal, which would allow users (employees) to submit help desk tickets and other requests for their assigned device(s).
- Use the internal BIOS Name as the place where you assign your Asset ID; this is set using the system bootup configuration settings; you can also duplicate the Asset ID using the Windows Computer Name, through the System Properties settings. Similar settings are available for macOS and Linux.

Keep in mind that you only need to be concerned with the assets you own (hardware and software), and tracking software licenses for hosted services. You should have clear language in any contract with a CSP or ISP as far as responsibilities for whatever resources you are using. For example, let's say you have 30 employees who all use the Microsoft Office 365 subscription service and five employees who use hosted QuickBooks software. The CSP may be responsible for ensuring you have the correct number of active licenses. Still, you are responsible for ensuring that you don't exceed the number of authorized users and also for keeping track of which specific employees are assigned a license. As another example, your contract with an ISP may specify the number of public IP addresses assigned to your business and also the maximum number of internal, private

IP addresses allowed within your office network. The ISP would be responsible for the public addresses, and you would be responsible for managing the internal addresses.

The asset management software will perform most of the tasks through automated scans; however, it is also necessary to input certain information that is not captured by the online scans. This includes the purchase details for each item of hardware or software, as outlined in the table below. In addition, you will need to manually input data for any company devices that are not connected to the network. Ideally, a physical inventory should be performed and compared with the purchase records and the automated software inventory. There is a template in Appendix D for doing a physical asset inventory. Once the three data sources have been reconciled for the first time, you should only need to repeat the full inventory process annually or every other year.

IT Asset Management – Purchase Information	
Hardware	**Software**
Purchase date	Purchase date
Purchase location (vendor)	Purchase location (vendor)
Unit cost (per device)	Unit cost (per license)
Model number/name	Total cost (multi-license package)
Serial number	Software title and version
Short item description	License key(s)
Standard or extended warranty service	Perpetual license or subscription service

Table 12-1. Purchase Information

The details available for any particular asset within an asset management system will vary between software applications; however, there is some basic information about both hardware and software that should be captured and maintained, at a minimum. That information starts with the purchase data given above, then includes the minimum attributes at the top of the table below. It may also include the optional attributes at the bottom of the table.

IT Asset Management – Minimum Attributes (Owned Assets)	
Hardware	**Software**
Asset ID (number or name)	Software title and version
Manufacturer and model	Number of licenses
Serial number	List of license keys
MAC address	(assigned and unassigned)
Assigned user (name)	License expiration date (if applicable)
(may include a title and phone number)	Software subscription renewal date
Assigned location (office space or mobile)	(if applicable)
Date placed in service	Asset IDs where software is installed
Associated peripheral device(s)	
Make, model, and serial number	
(display monitors, external drives, etc.)	
Assigned software (title and version)	
with date installed and license	
number/key	
Optional Asset Attributes	
Asset purpose (primary usage)	Technical support agreement
Internal IP address	(contact information and renewal date)
CPU (type, speed, and number)	
Amount of RAM (in GB)	
Number and size of internal storage drives	
Third-party support contract	
(contact information and renewal date)	
Assigned groups (for access control)	
Anti-Malware software	
(vendor and version)	

Table 12-2. Minimum Attributes

Implementing Sub-Controls 1.6 (Address unauthorized assets) and 2.6 (Address unapproved software)

You may rely on the asset management inventory for operational purposes, such as discovering unauthorized hardware devices or software. In the case of finding unauthorized hardware or software, you should include procedures in your security policies for addressing how to request that those items be placed on the "approved" list for your business. Employees found to have unauthorized hardware or software should be informed of the procedure. If authorized, they become part of the approved inventory (or an authorized personal device). If not authorized, then they must be removed from your computing environment and the employee notified appropriately. Your policy and enforcement stance will determine whether or not the unauthorized device or software is allowed to remain active during the approval review period.

Implementing Sub-Control 2.2 (Ensure software is supported by the vendor)

For Sub-Control 2.2, the last in this category, you will need to perform a manual check with each software vendor to ensure that the version of their software that you are using is still covered by their support agreement. Normally, you can set up software packages to perform automatic checks for updates whenever the application is launched, and this helps keep the product up to date. One consideration on this point is whether you have the application running centrally from a server or if it runs separately on individual computer systems. If it's on a server, you only need to configure the automatic updates in one place. If it runs locally on several different computer systems, then each one will need to be configured.

Implementing IG1 Sub-Controls for Basic System Administration (9 of 12 Sub-Controls)

Because the nature of the tasks performed for basic system administration and configuration management requires system-level administrative access, there are a few preparatory steps you should take.

- In compliance with Sub-Control 4.3, ensure that each person performing these tasks is using a dedicated administrative account.
- Tasks that will be automated (run without human intervention) should have their own dedicated administrative

account, configured with login disabled. This means the patch management software can use a system-level account from one machine to another to run scans and install patches, but a person could not use those credentials to login to a device. There should also be a separate account for the backup system.

- Ensure that all workstations, laptops, and tablets have a standard Administrator account on the local device, using a strong password.

- You will need to know the Administrative login credentials for other network or security devices that will be accessed for patching and updates.

- Ensure that any unique and separate devices used strictly for administrative tasks (such as a dedicated security workstation) are physically secure from unauthorized access, including theft or damage.

Implementing Sub-Controls 3.4 (Deploy automated operating system patch management tools) and 3.5 (Deploy automated software patch management tools)

<u>Patches vs. Updates</u>. You need to understand the difference between patch management and software updates or upgrades. Patches are intermediate releases of software code that fix ("patch") a known problem or error, especially those that create a security vulnerability. Patches are not intended to add or modify features or functionality of the software package, beyond just fixing the problem. Updates are considered to be enhancements to software features or functionality at the sub-version level – for example, an update from version 2.3 to version 2.5, which adds a new reporting function. Upgrades are considered to be the release of a new version of the software – for example, an upgrade from version 4.0 to version 5.0, which provides a whole set of new features or functions.

Patch management should be ongoing and occur daily or weekly. Updates and upgrades should be scheduled in advance (possibly quarterly or semi-annually), and the software should be tested before implementing them. While security patching may be set up to run automatically, you should not ignore software updates or upgrades because older and outdated software will become more vulnerable over time.

The easiest way to implement patch management for Sub-Controls 3.4 and 3.5 is to activate the automatic update feature for the operating systems and in each application, where available. This can be done on individual devices, or it can be done using a centralized GPO setting for the OS in those environments controlled through Active Directory. The setting should include critical and important updates. For centralized patch management, you should consider using either a free or paid version of patch management software and assess whether or not such a tool is compatible with your asset management software. Most solutions offer both a hosted cloud service and a local, on-site version, although the cloud service is usually not free.

You should be aware that the free versions have limitations of 25 to 50 devices. If you have more than 50 devices, then you would need to obtain the paid version. If you are considering a paid version of patch management software, the key factors at that point will be the cost and ease of use, since most of the features tend to be similar. Also, consider how much technical support is provided.

Implementing Sub-Control 8.2 (Ensure anti-malware software and signatures are updated)

Regardless of what anti-malware software you use, to achieve Sub-Control 8.2 you need to enable automatic updates for the malware signatures (on a continuous basis) and for the software itself (daily or weekly). This is a standard setting in almost every anti-malware package that should be enabled by default. If you don't have centralized device management, then this must be set on each device individually; otherwise, it can be set from a centralized console. This is one of the configuration settings that you should regularly verify is functioning correctly, at least once or twice per month.

Implementing Sub-Control 9.4 (Apply host-based firewalls or port-filtering)

For Sub-Control 9.4, you can use the built-in Windows Firewall or a firewall that comes bundled with your anti-malware software. There are several free and paid firewall packages available. You can generally use the default settings; however, it is recommended that you use a default "deny all" setting and then only allow explicitly authorized connections. This mainly concerns external connections and not sending data between computers within your office, which would be considered trusted connections.

Secondly, either through the local-host firewall or using another port-filtering tool, or even the command line interface (CLI), you should ensure that all unused ports are blocked and closed. Computer services (such as remote access) use certain logical ports, and if those services are not needed or not in use, leaving those ports open provides a means for a cyberattack. If possible, it is best to manage the port settings globally from a centralized console. If that is not available, then each device must be configured separately using an Administrator account.

Implementing Sub-Controls 10.1 (Ensure regular automated backups), 10.2 (Perform complete system backups), 10.4 (Protect backups), and 10.5 (Ensure all backups have at least one offline backup destination)

Creating back-up copies of your files is one of the core best practices for business continuity and disaster recovery. Whether you store most of your data locally on your own computers or it is stored in a cloud service, the back-up principles are the same. You should have three copies of each back-up, using at least two different types of back-up media (e.g., internal hard drive and portable hard drive), and having one copy stored securely off-site. Meeting the security measures for these four Sub-Controls (10.1, 10.2, 10.4, and 10.5) should be part of the standard operating procedures for any business.

This first set of actions pertain to businesses that store data on their own systems, either within their own office space or hosted at a data center.

- Have a back-up strategy or plan

  o Identify what data should be backed up and where it is stored

- Identify your back-up devices or destinations (use at least two types)

  o Back-up server (internal hard drives)
  o External hard drive(s) – attached to individual systems or centrally located
  o Cloud storage (separate location from operational data)

- Install the necessary back-up devices and software

  o Identify secure locations for back-up devices (physical security)
  o Identify authorized back-up administrators (digital security)

- Create a back-up schedule

  o Transactional data should be backed up incrementally on a daily basis (this captures files or data that have changed since the last back-up)
  o Full back-ups of critical systems should occur weekly or bi-weekly

- o Full back-ups of non-critical systems should occur monthly

- Create a system image back-up of a "master" workstation with a "clean," secure configuration and store it in a locked, fire-proof cabinet

  - o A system image back-up should be done for each different "master" configuration (for example, laptops using WiFi will have different settings than a desktop workstation on a wired connection)

- Create duplicate back-up copies for redundancy

  - o Primary back-up is located on the back-up device (e.g., back-up server drives)
  - o Secondary back-up is located on a removable hard drive and stored offline in a locked, fire-proof cabinet
  - o Tertiary back-up should be located on a remote device, geographically separated from the primary back-up, for disaster recovery purposes

- Encrypt back-up data that is transmitted across the network, outside of your office local area network (LAN); all external back-up storage devices should also be encrypted

  - o Confidential or sensitive information that is normally encrypted and protected from unauthorized access should be further encrypted on the back-up device (the original, encrypted files are usually backed up)

- Verify that back-ups are occurring correctly by performing data restoration periodically (i.e., monthly), to validate that the data which is supposed to be backed up is actually being backed up and that it is recoverable in usable form

- Consider using the Windows File History function on local systems to provide an easy way for users to retrieve files or prior versions of a file

  o This requires a separate drive from the one where the data is stored; it can be a second drive partition on a single physical drive, or it can be a second hard drive (either internal or external)

Several of the back-up steps above will also pertain to businesses that store the majority of their data in a cloud service. These additional actions apply to cloud storage situations:

- Understand your cloud services agreement and ensure that there is a provision for the CSP to back-up your data; otherwise, ensure that you have sufficient access to perform your own back-ups
- Ensure that your cloud service agreement has a provision for the CSP to provide you with a physical copy of your back-up data on a weekly or bi-weekly basis, or else full access to your back-up data so that you can make a copy
- Have the CSP provide periodic validation and verification of the success of the data back-ups, including data restoration

Implementing Sub-Control 16.11 (Lock workstation sessions after inactivity)

For Sub-Control 16.11, you basically configure all systems to activate the screen saver after a designated period of time and require a password to unlock it. Your security policy should state the time period for the length of inactivity before the screen saver turns on. You should base this time period on your business requirements; however, we recommend a maximum of thirty (30) minutes and, in general, a standard period of ten (10) or fifteen (15) minutes. You don't want to hinder work performance; for example, if the employee simply answers a phone call and stops using the computer for a short time, then returns to work on the computer.

This setting can be accomplished in a couple of ways. You can use a local security object on each computer, which would require any changes to be done manually on each system. If you are using Active Directory or another centralized device or user management tool, then you can create a GPO at the domain level and assign it to all devices. You do not need to assign the GPO to users since it is the device that needs the protection.

Implementing IG1 Sub-Controls for Configuration and System Management (6 of 9 Sub-Controls)

Implementing Sub-Control 5.1 (Establish secure configurations)

One part of completing Sub-Control 5.1 is documenting the configuration settings for each operating system. The other part is actually implementing the configuration settings and making a system backup of a "master" that can be used to create new systems or to restore one that has been corrupted. The master backup should be stored in a locked, fire-proof cabinet to prevent theft or damage. This secure configuration includes settings identified in other Sub-Controls, as well as some that are not. Here is a list of several items that should be part of the secure configuration (this list does not include every configuration setting):

- Enable automatic updates for the operating system
- Install and enable anti-malware protection, including automatic updates and scanning removable media
- Enable a local-host firewall, with a default rule to deny-all and only permit authorized connections
- Disable the autoplay function when removable media are connected or inserted

- Disable or block all unused ports (this might be done through the firewall)
- Disable any services that are not needed
- Set the screen saver to fifteen (15) minutes and require a password to unlock it
- If business data is stored on a particular system, then enable scheduled backups
- If sensitive or confidential data is stored on a particular system, then implement either full-disk encryption or folder/file encryption

Implementing Sub-Control 7.1 (Ensure use of only fully supported browsers and email clients)

For Sub-Control 7.1, you should first establish standards for the web browser, email client, and other office software for your business. Then, periodically check with the software vendors to confirm the versions they are supporting. Most vendors will support the current version plus two prior versions. You should only need to update versions once a year.

Implementing Sub-Control 7.7 (Use of DNS filtering services)

While configuring and managing the use of Domain Name Services (DNS) can require some more intermediate skills, for Sub-Control 7.7, there is a free DNS filtering service called Quad9 (https://www.quad9.net) that was created jointly by the Global Cyber Alliance, IBM, and the Packet Clearing House. Quad9 is easy to implement and blocks malicious websites from being accessed by your web browsers and other systems.

Implementing Sub-Control 8.4 (Configure anti-malware scanning of removable media)

For Sub-Control 8.4, you should be able to set a standard configuration option in the anti-malware settings that will scan any removable media (such as USB drives) any time they are plugged into the computer. Some packages have an additional option to scan the removable media anytime a file is opened from or saved to the device.

Implementing Sub-Control 8.5 (Configure devices to not auto-run content)

There is a configuration setting in the Windows system properties that is used to achieve Sub-Control 8.5. On individual computers, within the system settings, select "Devices" and then select the "Autoplay" option. Be sure the setting is "off." If you are using Active Directory or another centralized device management tool, you can set this parameter default for all devices.

Implementing Sub-Control 15.7 (Leverage the Advanced Encryption Standard (AES) to encrypt wireless data)

To implement Sub-Control 15.7, you need to configure your wireless router (also called a wireless access point or WAP), so that it requires the AES encryption standard. This setting might also need to be set or confirmed on any portable device that uses the wireless connection.

Chapter 13

Implementing User Controls and Training

With administrative and configuration Sub-Controls in place, now it's time to move on to securing the workforce. We start with user account security and then move on to awareness and training.

Implementing IG1 Sub-Controls for User Administration (4 of 4 Sub-Controls)

Implementing Sub-Control 4.2 (Change default passwords)

Whenever you install a new device or software that comes with a default password – usually an administrative one to facilitate installation – you should change it immediately. You can often make the change during the installation process, although in some cases it will be after the installation is complete. Make sure the new password follows your policy for password minimum length and strength; for example, a minimum of 15 characters, including upper- and lower-case letters, along with either numbers or special characters. As a quick side note – eight characters used to be the gold standard, but eight-character passwords are far too easy to crack with modern computers. I recommend at least 15 characters. Some older applications and web sites still use eight characters, but overwhelmingly those are for non-sensitive applications. If one of your application providers "maxes out" at eight characters, I urge you to consider that as a negative factor when contemplating replacement software.

If you are not able to change the default password on a particular device or software, create a separate administrative account (e.g.,

"Admin2") with an appropriate password, then disable the default account. An alternative security precaution is to also rename the default account, which is often "Admin," to a name that is less obvious.

Implementing Sub-Control 4.3 (Ensure the use of dedicated administrative accounts)

One of your security policies should specify that any administrative-level login access to your computer systems should be through an assigned administrative user account. Only those employees who are authorized for system-level access should have this type of account, and it should be used exclusively for performing system administration tasks. These authorized employees should always use their regular login credentials for doing other daily tasks on their computers, and those regular user accounts should not have administrative access rights. User account naming conventions can be simple – for example, standard users might be identified by first initial, a period/dot, and last name, so that Jonathan Doe would be "j.doe." If Jonathan is an authorized system administrator, his administrative user account might be "j.doe.adm."

You should conduct periodic (e.g., monthly) reviews of the system log files to ensure that the administrative-level accounts are being used appropriately. In other words, that they are not being used for accessing email, Internet surfing, playing games, or any other non-administrative tasks.

Implementing Sub-Controls 16.8 (Disable any unassociated accounts) and 16.9 (Disable dormant accounts)

Your security policy should dictate that each employee (or other authorized system user) has a unique User ID that is associated only with that one individual. Therefore, you should check all of the created user accounts to ensure each one is linked to a single person or to a unique system process and disable those that are not. This check and disable process should be done on a regular basis (e.g., monthly). Performing backups is an example of a unique system process. This process requires administrative-level access to drives and file systems and is not usually assigned to a particular person.

At the same time as you check for unassociated user accounts, you should also check for valid accounts that have not been used for an extended period of time (called a dormant account). You should set this time period in your security policy based on your business situation. For example, if employees are allowed a two-week vacation, then possibly set the time period for 21 days, or have a general period of 30 or 60 days before an account is deemed dormant. Dormant accounts should be disabled to prevent unauthorized access and, when the employee returns, the account will have to be re-enabled. If the employee does not return the account remains disabled, and all access rights should also be removed.

Implementing IG1 Sub-Controls for Awareness and Training (6 of 6 Sub-Controls)

Implementing Sub-Control 17.3 (Implement a security awareness program)

For Sub-Control 17.3, you just need to create the cybersecurity awareness and training program outlined in the book, using the template from Appendix D. Start with the training sessions, then work your way into creating awareness materials and methods of delivery.

Implementing Sub-Controls 17.5 (Train workforce on secure authentication), 17.6 (Train workforce on identifying social engineering attacks), 17.7 (Train workforce on sensitive data handling), 17.8 (Train workforce on causes of unintentional data exposure), and 17.9 (Train workforce on identifying and reporting incidents)

Training on the five topics listed for Sub-Controls 17.5 – 17.9 can be accomplished in a single session lasting approximately 90 minutes. The following paragraphs summarize the content for each topic area.

Secure authentication should be covered in your cybersecurity policies. Each employee (or other person) who is authorized to log in to your company's computer systems must have a User ID that is unique to that individual and create a strong password. In some places, companies might use biometrics (fingerprint or retinal scan) for higher levels of security. The process of authentication is intended to validate the user who is accessing company computing resources. Employees or other users should never share or disclose their login credentials with anyone and should not keep them written down anywhere around their workstation.

Social engineering is one of the most common tactics used in cyberattacks. Tricking a person into revealing login credentials or releasing other sensitive information is easier than trying to forcefully hack into a computer system. Social engineering consists of criminals using various combinations of tactics, techniques, and methods. Any of these actions, by itself, may not indicate a potential attack; however, if several of these actions are combined and focused on one or a few employees, there is a strong likelihood that it is a social engineering attack.

Social engineering tactics include the following, escalating from least obtrusive to openly criminal acts:

- befriending someone to gain their trust

- using persuasion
- using trickery or deceit
- using intimidation
- using coercion or threats
- using extortion or blackmail

Social engineering techniques can include the following, used separately or in combination:

- urgency – something has to be done now
- quid pro quo – I'll do something for you, if you do this for me
- kindness – I'm just doing this to help you...
- position – I'm your boss (or another company manager), so do as I say

Social engineering methods include the following, generally used separately based on the circumstances:

- shoulder surfing – either looking over someone's shoulder in person or by the use of hidden cameras
- dumpster diving – checking the trash for discarded information
- piggy-backing – following employees into a locked facility
- phishing or spear-phishing – targeted email messages that appear legitimate
- role-playing – pretending to be someone they are not (e.g., "I'm from Tech Support")

Proper <u>handling of sensitive or confidential information</u> should be straight-forward. First, only those employees who are authorized to view sensitive information as part of their required job duties should have access to it. This includes both online access and paper documents. Protecting the information while viewing it includes having the display monitor facing away from open areas where an unauthorized person might be able to view it. Alternately, there are filter panels that fit over a display monitor that block viewing from any angle, except sitting directly in front of the monitor screen. Another protection measure is to remove any sensitive information from the display monitor whenever the employee leaves their workspace. In addition, to prevent unauthorized access to their computer, they should also activate the screen saver (with a password needed to clear it) before leaving their workspace.

There are many ways an employee might <u>unintentionally release sensitive information</u> to an unauthorized person, or at least expose the information without proper protection. The following are just a few examples:

- Let's start with paper documents containing sensitive information – an employee could forget to lock them in a cabinet when leaving for lunch or going home at the end of the day. At that point, anyone could walk up to that employee's desk and read or take the documents.

- For digital records, the company may not have a written policy for locking a workstation after a period of inactivity (or related Group Policy Object to automate the process) and an employee leaves sensitive information on their screen when leaving for lunch or going home at the end of the day. As a result, anyone could walk up and view the information, as well as potentially download or copy sensitive data onto a portable storage device (i.e., thumb drive).

- An employee from human resources may need to send workers' compensation information about an injured employee to their insurance company and accidentally sends it as an attachment to a non-encrypted email message.

- A particular workgroup uses shared storage through a cloud service, and instead of being properly configured to restrict access to only the users in the workgroup, the settings are actually configured so that the files and data can be found and accessed through a web browser search by anyone.

Once employees learn <u>how to identify a potential cyberattack</u>, they also need to know the proper <u>procedure for reporting it</u>. Your security policy should address when, how, and where employees should report suspicious computer activity. At first, it is probably better to get too many reports and weed out those that are not valid. Then, you can start to fine-tune the criteria or circumstances for WHEN employees should report something. The HOW and WHERE to make a report should remain constant – identify a contact person (or Help Desk, if applicable) and provide a phone number and email address.

Tell employees not to send any potentially malicious files, unless specifically instructed to do so by the person or security team responsible for accepting the report. Employees should make a note of their actions just prior to discovering a potential cyberattack, and also what occurred on the computer (if anything) that was not normal. This would include such things as the mouse cursor moving around the screen by itself, the desktop background has changed, or an unknown web page appears when the browser is opened – none of which are being done by the employee. Other indications include receiving a ransom demand to unlock your files, or when one or more systems have extremely slow response times, even for simple tasks such as opening a two-page document. Whoever is responsible for receiving reports of potential cyberattacks must be prepared to give instructions to the reporting employee for whatever actions might be necessary.

Chapter 14

Implementing Incident and Breach Controls

With infrastructure and workforce Sub-Controls in place, now it's time to move on to securing your sensitive data and preparing for incidents and breaches.

Implementing IG1 Sub-Controls for Protecting Sensitive or Confidential Information (3 of 3 Sub-Controls)

Implementing Sub-Control 13.1 (Maintain an inventory of sensitive information)

This task may seem daunting at first, but you don't need to inventory the individual data items for Sub-Control 13.1, you just need to inventory the places where the data is stored, used, and transmitted. Most sensitive information is going to be kept in a database, usually managed through an application. You need to know what it is and where it is kept. Even if the data is stored and protected by a CSP, it is still your data, and you need to identify it as part of your inventory.

- Identify the type(s) of sensitive data you store, use, or maintain (under your control)
  - customers' personal information, including billing or payment information
  - employees' personnel records
  - proprietary or trade secrets

- Identify where the databases are located (where the data is stored)

- o   servers or workstations within your offices
- o   servers you own and manage, hosted at another facility
- o   servers hosted by a CSP

- Identify who uses the data and on which workstations or other devices
- Determine if there are paper copies of the data that need protecting
- Identify whether the data travels across any public network segments or only within your local office network, and be aware of wireless networks

  - o   All sensitive data should be encrypted when sent across any network

Implementing Sub-Control 13.2 (Remove sensitive data on systems not regularly accessed by the organization)

This Sub-Control 13.2 should be fairly easy and straight-forward. Any computer system that contains sensitive information and is not regularly used for accessing that information should have all of the sensitive data removed. Use a data erasure tool that "wipes" the data from the drive. Do not simply use the delete function because that only erases the file indexing information and leaves most of the data intact. Perform periodic checks of workstations, laptops, and other devices to ensure that there is no sensitive data where it doesn't belong.

Implementing Sub-Control 13.6 (Encrypt mobile device data)

For Sub-Control 13.6, you should encrypt the data storage media on all mobile devices. For workstations and laptops, you can use the Windows BitLocker tool or another encryption tool. For other mobile devices, such as tablets and smartphones, you will need to use a tool that works with the device's operating system (e.g., Android or iOS). It is best to configure the device to encrypt the entire drive, and you can still encrypt individual files as necessary. Have a safe and secure place to store the encryption key (password) and be sure not to lose it.

Implementing IG1 Sub-Controls for Incident Response Management (4 of 4 Sub-Controls)

One key element of incident response management is documentation. You want to have a record of what happened and capture any potential evidence (e.g., copies of malware or phishing email messages with malicious web links) so that the incident can be resolved.

Implementing Sub-Control 19.1 (Document incident response procedures)

For Sub-Control 19.1, use the template in Appendix D to create your cybersecurity incident response plan and procedures, customizing it to meet your small business needs. The template provides more details about taking action and documentation, rather than using the simple checklist.

Implementing Sub-Control 19.3 (Designate management personnel to support incident handling)

For Sub-Control 19.3, use the information from the template in Appendix D as a guideline for the roles and responsibilities that need to be designated for incident response. You should have one primary point of contact who will be in charge of managing incident response. Also, designate an alternate person, in case the primary person is not available or able to perform the necessary duties. These should ideally be management-level employees who provide guidance to other staff who are performing the necessary response tasks.

Implementing Sub-Control 19.5 (Maintain contact information for reporting security incidents)

There are two categories of people or external organizations you want to have available. First are the names, phone numbers, and email addresses for anyone outside of your business who will be part of the response team. This usually includes someone at your ISP or CSP, or another third-party security contractor, and might also include your local law enforcement agency, if they offer assistance to small businesses during a cyberattack. Second are the names, phone numbers, and email addresses of those people who will be part of a legal response to a cyberattack. This includes your own legal counsel, your local law enforcement agency's computer crime unit, the closest FBI computer crime squad, and your cyber insurance carrier.

There are two ways to proceed if you simply want to report a cyber incident without asking for immediate law enforcement assistance. You can contact your local police department or sheriff's office to report the potential crime, or you can file a report with the Internet Crime Complaint Center (IC3) at https://www.ic3.gov/. Before contacting law enforcement, and possibly your insurance carrier, you might want to consult with your legal counsel and let them coordinate the notifications.

You can meet the requirements of Sub-Control 19.5 by maintaining (and keeping updated) a list of the following external contacts, as applicable, related to cybersecurity incident response, in addition to having a list of the internal response team.

- Your ISP – security operations for incident response (separate from customer service)
- Your CSP – security operations for incident response (separate from customer service)
- Any third-party contractors who provide security services for your small business

- Local law enforcement – cybercrime unit, if possible, otherwise ask them who should be your contact
- Regional FBI field office – cybercrime squad
- Government agencies that regulate your industry
- Your cyber insurance carrier

Implementing Sub-Control 19.6 (Publish information regarding computer anomalies and incidents)

For Sub-Control 19.6, your cybersecurity awareness and training program should be helping employees to recognize what constitutes a "cyber incident." They should understand what should be reported to the contact person for the internal incident response team, and also what does not need to be reported. Have them err on the side of reporting potential incidents, and for those that turn out not to be valid, use them as training events to provide a better understanding of why it wasn't a valid incident. The instructions for employees to report cybersecurity incidents should be posted in a common area (such as work room, lunchroom or break room, conference room) and made available electronically on a company Intranet site or shared network folder. It may be helpful to provide employees with a simple form to capture basic information from them regarding what they are reporting.

Congratulations - You made it through all of the background materials and the steps to create your cybersecurity program. There are two key points worth repeating, which should lead to long-term success for your program!

1. IT and cybersecurity should be enablers, not hindrances, of your business processes and operations, and it sometimes takes an effort to keep them that way. It is possible for business innovation and flexibility to occur, even within a secure computing environment, as long as everyone remembers the purpose of the security program and doesn't try to undermine or bypass the controls you put in place.

2. A good cybersecurity awareness program will go a long way to having employees incorporate safe computing habits into their daily work duties, and help create a cyber-secure work culture. Rather than focusing on the punitive nature of violating policies, the awareness program should encourage and reward employees for doing the right things to protect the company information assets, including customer information.

Appendix A

Glossary of Terms and Acronyms

Two primary sources of definitions for terms and acronyms related to cybersecurity were used in this book:

1. NIST Interagency/Internal Report (NIST-IR) #7298 R2 (May 2013) *

   https://nvlpubs.nist.gov/nistpubs/ir/2013/NIST.IR.729 8r2.pdf

2. Committee on National Security Systems Instructions (CNSSI) #4009 (April 2015) *

* Both original sources will soon be deprecated and replaced with a new online reference at: https://csrc.nist.gov/glossary

While some of the following terms or phrases may be defined in other places, for the purposes of this book, they have the meanings and definitions provided below.

Accountability – means that action taken within a computer system, especially administrative or configuration changes, are tracked and logged, and that each action is attributable to a particular user.

ACL (Access Control List) – pertains to a list of devices, network addresses, users or other objects that are assigned either "allow" or "deny" permission to access designated resources or networks; most often used in firewalls and routers.

Administrative Account – sometimes also referred to as a "System Account," this type of login account has elevated privileges above regular user accounts, to perform administrative tasks on the computer system, such as managing other user accounts, allowing or denying access to file storage locations, performing system backup and recovery, installing or deleting applications, and other tasks requiring access to the core operating system functions.

Administrative Controls – one of the three main categories of risk management controls; this one is used to govern human behaviors, through policies and regulations directing employees' actions, either in what they must perform or what is prohibited. (refer to Operational Controls and Technical Controls)

Anomaly-Based Detection – refers to the method of detecting a potential cyber intrusion by using a baseline of "normal" activity and comparing current, ongoing network and system activity to determine any anomalous behavior. See also, Signature-Based Detection.

Asset – refers to an item deemed to have value to an organization, which may have negative impacts to the operation of the organization if it were to be stolen, damaged or inaccessible; assets, in general, may be physical equipment (e.g., hardware, machinery, etc.), digital (e.g., application or web software, database, etc.) or intangible (e.g., copyright, trademark, intellectual property, etc.).

Authentication – the process of allowing system login for a specified user; it does not provide permissions to use/access any system resources (see Authorization); authentication can be applied to single computers or the company network as a larger resource.

Authorization – the permissions given to a group or individual user to access or use specified system resources or assets; for example, permission to access a folder on a shared file storage device, which may include the rights for read-only (view), write (create), modify or delete; another example is permission to use the company's email system, but not the human resources application.

Baseline Security – refers to the minimum set of security control measures to protect an information asset, based on the specific IT system's confidentiality, integrity, and availability requirements.

BC/DR (Business Continuity / Disaster Recovery) – refers to two business-related planning activities and their related business plans (Business Continuity Plan and Disaster Recovery Plan), which address two aspects of emergency response to a disaster, whether natural or man-made; the Business Continuity Plan covers how the business should function at a minimum level for the duration of a disaster and should also address when the business should shut down its operations; the Disaster Recovery Plan covers what the business must do to re-start operations and get back to a normal operating level after the disaster has ended; both plans must take into account the safety of employees critical equipment, as well as what job functions will continue to be performed and which ones will be temporarily discontinued.

Blacklisting – refers to a process to identify and list software programs, users, network addresses or web sites (URL addresses) that are not authorized to execute or launch on an information system.

BIA (Business Impact Analysis) – refers to an analysis of one or more information systems' functions, requirements, and interdependencies (with other systems and with business operations), to characterize system contingency requirements and priorities in the event the system becomes unavailable.

C.I.A. (Confidentiality, Integrity, Availability) – known as the Triad of Cybersecurity; the ultimate goal of security measures and controls is to protect information assets' *Confidentiality* (only those authorized to access the information are able to access it), *Integrity* (assurance that the information has not been altered or deleted), and *Availability* (the information is accessible by authorized individuals when it is needed).

CIS (Center for Internet Security) – CIS a 501(c)3 non-profit organization whose mission is to identify, develop, validate, promote, and sustain best practices in cybersecurity; deliver world-class cybersecurity solutions to prevent and rapidly respond to cyber incidents; and build and lead communities to enable an environment of trust in cyberspace.

Cloud Computing – refers to the use of applications or other services hosted by a Cloud Service Provider, as opposed to computing resources and services owned and operated by a local business. Examples of Cloud Computing include (1) the use of Salesforce.com for managing customer information and communications, (2) using Microsoft Office365 for general productivity (Word, Excel, email, etc.), or (3) using Google Drive for file storage and backup.

Compensating Security Control – refers to the security controls (i.e., safeguards or countermeasures) implemented by an organization in lieu of using recommended controls from NIST or other standards, and that provide equivalent or comparable protection.

Countermeasure(s) – refers to the protective measures taken to meet security requirements (i.e., confidentiality, integrity, and availability), which may include actions, devices, procedures, techniques or other measures to reduce vulnerabilities; synonymous with security controls and safeguards.

Credentials or **Electronic Credentials** – refers, in general, to the User ID and password combination for each authorized user; it may also include other methods of authentication, such as biometrics or a smart card.

CSC (Critical Security Controls) – refers to the set of 20 critical cybersecurity controls published by CIS, last revised in April 2019 with CIS Controls® version 7.1.

CSF (Cybersecurity Framework) – refers to the NIST "Framework for Improving Critical Infrastructure Cybersecurity" ver. 1.1, issued in April 2018.

CSIRT (Cyber Security Incident Response Team) – refers to the formalized or ad hoc group that is responsible for security incident response and recovery; team members are usually from cross-functional areas of the organization; responsible for identifying the cause and type of incident, halting any further incursion or compromise, eradicating any malware, restoring systems to normal operations, and reporting to management.

Cyber Hygiene – refers to the principle of taking simple, basic actions to provide minimal levels of security, such as operating system automated patching, using anti-malware software that is automatically updated, backing up your data to a secure location, using a basic firewall and configuring applications (e.g., web browser) with basic security settings, and having secure login credentials.

FIPS (Federal Information Processing Standard) – refers to the standards published by NIST for federal agencies to adopt, including guidelines and requirements for security and interoperability, where there are no acceptable industry standards.

IAM (Identity and Access Management) – refers to the combined practice of managing identities (user accounts) and their permissions to access certain resources (which may include physical facilities and computer systems).

IBAC (Identity-Based Access Control) – refers to the practice and model of controlling access to resources based on the user's identity; see also Role-Based Access Control (RBAC).

IDS (Intrusion Detection System) – refers to a security device or software that scans real-time network traffic and/or system activity and provides alerts when it detects suspicious activity; there are two, mutually exclusive types of IDS, network-based which monitors network traffic, and host-based which monitors activity on a server or other local device; methods of detection include signature-based, where activity is compared with a database of known attacks, and anomaly-based, where activity is compared with a configured baseline.

Impact Value – Sometimes referred to as "Severity," this is the monetary value a business assigns to the tangible and intangible business impacts if a particular asset is compromised. Impacts include, but is not limited to, direct monetary loss (theft), loss of revenue, loss of business reputation, loss of customers, and the costs to halt and remediate a cyber-attack.

Information Asset – refers to information or data which is valuable to the organization and should be protected; usually means digital information, but also applies to paper and other formats.

IPS (Intrusion Prevention System) – a security system that can be either a network-based device or host-based software; it monitors network traffic or monitors activity on the host computer, watching for data packets that match known malware signatures, or for anomalous activity that varies from the configured baseline, which indicate a potential attack or breach, then automatically takes action to stop the attack.

The IPS is usually configured and fine-tuned within each environment, to reduce or eliminate false alarms.

Likelihood of Occurrence – Sometimes measured as the "Frequency of Occurrence," this is the probability of a particular vulnerability will be exploited by any particular threat, or how often a vulnerability will be exploited over a one-year period.

NGF or **NGFW** (**Next Generation Firewall**) – current, third-generation firewall technology that incorporate advanced features beyond typical filtering, including stateful packet inspection, which allow network traffic to be managed not only using IP addresses, ports, and protocols, but also perform deep packet inspection, application-level firewall functions, web application firewall functions, and may provide additional security functions, such as intrusion detection and prevention.

NIST (**National Institute of Standards and Technology**) – the federal agency (within the U.S. Department of Commerce) responsible for creating cybersecurity standards and guidelines, which are generally mandatory for all U.S. government agencies, as well as private companies under government contracts. Otherwise, the standards provide private businesses with a common set of security measures, most of which are mapped to other regulatory standards, such as HIPAA (Health Insurance Portability and Accountability Act) and PCI-DSS (Payment Card Industry Data Security Standards).

Operational Controls – one of the three main categories of risk management controls; this one is used to guide daily operations; these are the manual or automated procedures and processes that ensure certain security tasks are performed in a specified manner and sequence. (refer to Administrative Controls and Technical Controls)

Penetration Testing – refers to a methodology and practice of conducting security testing under well-defined and controlled conditions, using attempts to bypass or overcome security measures in an organization's network and servers; the purpose is to identify gaps and weaknesses in existing security measures so they can be fixed.

Risk – refers to the measure of the extent to which a particular threat may take advantage of exploiting a vulnerability in the organization's network or computing systems; security risks may result in the loss of confidentiality, integrity or availability of information assets; the severity of a risk affects the potential impact to the organization, in combination with the likelihood of the risk occurring.

RBAC (Role-Based Access Control) – refers to the practice and model of assigning system permissions and access rights based on a system role, which can equate to a job function, rather than assigning rights based on individual identities; see also Identity-Based Access Control (IBAC).

Security Control Assessment – refers to the testing and evaluation of the administrative, operational, and technical security controls, to determine the extent to which the controls are properly or improperly implemented, functioning as intended, and producing the desired outcomes in protecting the confidentiality, integrity, and availability of an organization's information assets.

Security Testing or **Security Audit** – refers to an independent examination and review of system records and activities, using internal or external auditors, to determine the adequacy of security controls to meet the goals and requirements of the organization's security policies and procedures, as well as any regulatory requirements, and provide recommendations for changes or improvements in the security controls. Security testing may also include a review of the organization's policies and procedures, including BC/DR plans and incident management plan.

Signature-Based Detection – refers to a method of detecting potential malware or other types of intrusions based on a database of known "signatures" of malicious software and intrusions; most often used in Intrusion Detection/Prevention Systems and Anti-Malware software, when scanning current network or system activity. See also, Anomaly-Based Detection.

Technical Controls – one of the three main categories of risk management controls; this one uses technology to manage risk, these are the security devices and software, setup to defend against cyber-attacks, as well as monitoring for signs of compromise; this includes the proper placement and configuration settings of key security components that perform automated security tasks. (refer to Administrative Controls and Operational Controls)

Threat – refers to an event, incident, condition or circumstance that has the potential for causing the loss of an asset or to adversely impact organizational operations, which may result from unauthorized access, damage or destruction of data, unauthorized disclosure, modification of data or denial of service; may also refer to the potential for a threat actor to exploit a known vulnerability.

Threat Actor – refers to an individual or group of individuals who are, in general, considered to be cyber criminals or others having malicious intent to take advantage of vulnerabilities in computer systems or networks belonging to others; this does not refer to artificial intelligence or other automated methods of attacking computer systems.

Vulnerability – refers to a weakness in an information system, security controls or implementation of security measures, or a flaw in software code, which could be exploited by a threat source.

Vulnerability Assessment – refers to a formal, systematic examination of information systems or networks to determine the presence of any vulnerabilities, including deficiencies in security measures or controls; using collected data to predict the effectiveness of such controls, and recommending remediation actions.

Whitelisting – refers to the process and list of designated devices, users, applications, and websites (URLs) that are authorized to launch or execute on an information system.

Appendix B

References and Small Business Resources

Author's NOTE: The links to web sites listed below were valid as of the publication date of this book. Please keep in mind that web links change over time and if one or more of the links below does not work, try a search on the organization's primary website for the related cybersecurity topic or document.

Center for Internet Security (CIS)

- CIS Controls v.7.1, April 2019

    o https://www.cisecurity.org/controls/

- CIS Controls v.7.1 – Implementation Groups

    o https://www.cisecurity.org/controls/cis-controls-implementation-groups/

- CIS Risk Assessment Method (CIS RAM) for CIS Controls v7

    o https://learn.cisecurity.org/cis-ram

- Measures and Metrics for CIS Controls v7, March 2018

    o https://www.cisecurity.org/white-papers/cis-controls-v7-measures-metrics/

Common Vulnerabilities and Exposures (CVE) Database

- Regularly updated listing of cybersecurity vulnerabilities

    o https://cve.mitre.org/cve/index.html

Federal Bureau of Investigation (FBI)

- What We Investigate – Cyber Crime

  o https://www.fbi.gov/investigate/cyber

- Internet Crime Complaint Center (IC3) – Report a Potential Cyber Crime

  o https://www.ic3.gov/default.aspx

Federal Communication Commission (FCC)

- "Cyber Planner 2.0" (build your own cybersecurity plan online)

  o https://www.fcc.gov/cyberplanner

Federal Trade Commission (FTC)

- Cybersecurity for Small Businesses (Consumer Protection)

  o https://www.ftc.gov/tips-advice/business-center/small-businesses/cybersecurity

National Institute of Standards and Technology (NIST)

- Interagency Report 7621 Rev. 1 (November 2016), "Small Business Information Security: The Fundamentals"

  o https://doi.org/10.6028/NIST.IR.7621r1

- Special Publication 800-30 Rev. 1 (September 2012), "Guide for Conducting Risk Assessments" [This would be an alternative to the CIS RAM.]

  o https://doi.org/10.6028/NIST.SP.800-30r1

- "Framework for Improving Critical Infrastructure Cybersecurity" v.1.1 (April 2018) [aka "Cybersecurity Framework" or "CSF"]

    o https://nvlpubs.nist.gov/nistpubs/CSWP/NIST.CSWP.04162018.pdf

- National Vulnerability Database (NVD)

    o https://nvd.nist.gov/General (Home page)
    o https://nvd.nist.gov/general/nvd-dashboard   (NVD Dashboard)
    o https://nvd.nist.gov/vuln/search (Vulnerability Search)

Small Business Administration (SBA)

- SBA Business Guide (general information resources under four areas: to Plan, Launch, Manage, & Grow your business)

    o https://www.sba.gov/business-guide

- SBA Learning Center: "Cybersecurity for small businesses" (30-minute tutorial)

    o https://www.sba.gov/course/cybersecurity-small-businesses/

- SCORE – SBA Technology Resources Partner (website contains 25 pages of informative links)

    o https://www.score.org/technology-resources

SANS Institute

- CIS Critical Security Controls (Training and Research)

    o https://www.sans.org/critical-security-controls/

- General Security Resources

- o https://www.sans.org/security-resources/

Stay Safe Online (National Cybersecurity Alliance)

- Small Business Resources Library
  - o https://staysafeonline.org/resources/?filter=.topic-cybersecure-my-business.resource-item
- CyberSecure My Business™
  - o https://staysafeonline.org/cybersecure-business/

Additional Resources for Small Businesses:

- CISO Desk Reference Guide - Small Business Series
  - o https://cisodrg.com/small-business/

Appendix C

Incorporating Cybersecurity Risks into a Business Risk Management Plan

Businesses generally calculate several different types of risk factors that may impact the success or failure of the business. These may include, for example:

- regional and national economic conditions
- ease of entry or barriers to entry into a particular market
- stability of the supply chain and availability of raw materials
- availability and scalability of distribution channels
- operating in a broad market vs. a niche market
- local environmental conditions (e.g., earthquake zone, flood plain, hurricane or tornado zone)
- the number and size of competing businesses, and their maturity/longevity in business

Also, a business operating in a regulated industry must consider compliance issues (e.g., HIPAA or PCI-DSS). No matter the individual circumstances for a particular business, there should be a risk analysis using all relevant factors. This allows the owners and management to make informed decisions about mitigating impacts and lowering overall business risk.

Here are some risk management terms you should know:

- Inherent Risk – this is the initial level of business risk, before applying any mitigation or security measures
- Residual Risk – this is the risk remaining after the application of mitigation or security measures; this risk level can change for a particular asset, as an iterative process of applying

mitigation and re-assessment, until the point of diminishing returns

- Acceptable Risk – this is the level of risk management is willing to accept without further mitigation or security measures being applied; note that this would be the lowest level of residual risk

Each business should have defined levels of acceptable risk, or at least the methods or principles to be used in achieving acceptable risk levels.

The business risk management plan should identify the four primary techniques of addressing risk, listed below, and when each method should be applied.

- Eliminate the risk – usually by removing the business condition that creates the risk. However, this could potentially include making changes to the internal or external environment, which removes the source of the risk.
- Mitigate the risk – taking steps to protect the business, secure the assets, build in contingencies and redundancies, and otherwise reduce the business impacts.
- Transfer the risk – having a third party take on most or all of the risk, most commonly by the use of insurance, or through contract terms (such as the security responsibilities for an Internet service provider or cloud services provider).
- Accept the risk – reaching a level of risk that management is willing to retain and accept without additional mitigation (e.g., the cost of additional security measures would be more than the value of the assets being protected).

Whether the risk management plan is a separate document or incorporated into the business plan, the business needs to incorporate cyber risks into the structure. This is equivalent to having an "all-hazards" perspective as part of an emergency management plan. In Chapter 4, we recommended using the CIS RAM tools to perform a risk assessment and assign risk values.

- Create a list of critical information assets by using the CIS RAM tools and prioritize them from high risk to low risk. The CIS RAM can be used for non-cyber risks as well. This list is necessary for performing an accurate risk assessment.

- If you don't already have a risk management plan, now is the time to create one, to include both business risks and cyber risks. Check the SBA resources in Appendix B for templates and other information.

- If you already have a risk management plan and have done basic business risk assessments, incorporate cyber risks into your assessments, using a prioritized list of your information assets that were assigned a medium- or high-risk value.

- The risk management plan should require both qualitative and quantitative analyses of high-priority assets, where each rating or ranking criteria has a clear definition.

- The risk management plan should specify that risk assessments are conducted on a regular, recurring basis. Cybersecurity risks should be assessed at least annually. Also, a cyber risk assessment should be performed when new systems are being implemented or major updates are being planned.

Basic Risk Assessment Considerations

To start the process of evaluating cybersecurity risk factors in relation to other business risk factors, you need to identify and understand areas of potential cybersecurity risk. You also need to identify the critical business assets and processes where cybersecurity risks will apply. As for determining a risk value for business assets using cybersecurity risk factors, the same basic formulas that are used for other types of risk factors will apply. There are some differences in the risk factors used for cyber risks that would not equate to the risk factors for other types of business risk, such as for physical facilities.

From a broad perspective, there are two main categories of risk – internal and external. Internal risks include financial risk, workforce risk, operational risk, and most cybersecurity risk. A company has more control over internal risk factors. External risk factors are generally outside of the control of a business, requiring more of a reactionary stance. These might include regulatory compliance, environmental conditions, national and global economics, availability of raw materials, and certain Internet cybersecurity risks.

When calculating the business impact of risks, you will need to know the value of an asset and the costs associated with a breach or system compromise. On the value side of the equation, start with the basic purchase costs of the hardware and software or the cost of the service contract with your Internet service provider or cloud services provider. Then, more importantly for your business, is the value of the data or information stored in or used by the asset, such as your customer database. This value calculation needs to determine what would happen to the business if that data or information is not available or has been corrupted.

On the cost side of the equation, you need to add together the costs for staff and other outside assistance for stopping a cyberattack, finding and remediating the source (e.g., removing malware from your systems), repairing damage to your systems (e.g., reinstalling software and restoring backup data), and restoring normal operations (e.g., ensuring that the most recent transactions have been accounted for). Part of these costs includes the monthly or annual fees or premiums you pay for outside security services and cyber insurance.

Example Risk Assessment Scenarios

For the remainder of this appendix, we will be using the example risk matrix shown in Figure C-1 below to work through some scenarios for calculating an asset's risk value. You may find variations of this matrix, ranging from 3x3 (nine boxes) to 10x10 (100 boxes).

This example risk matrix has been divided into four risk categories, as indicated by the different hashes. The hashes correlate to a risk level, where lower-left hash indicates low risk, next hash indicates medium-low risk, next indicates medium-high risk, and upper-right indicates high risk. This style is sometimes called a "heat map" because when rendered in color, the areas in the upper half of the diagonal are orange and red, considered "hot" targets with high risk. The boxes included in each category are determined by the risk tolerance of the organization. It may shift to the lower-left for more risk-averse companies, meaning there are more medium-high and high boxes risk boxes in the upper-right diagonal and fewer low and medium boxes in the lower-left diagonal. Or, it may shift to the upper-right for more risk-tolerant companies, with fewer medium-high and high boxes and more of the low and medium boxes.

Now, how would you use this matrix in your small business to start assigning risk values to your assets? Let's walk through a few example scenarios, so that you understand the process and how simple it can be. Of course, it can become more complex, depending on the level of detail and amount of analysis you want to do. When learning the risk assessment process, it is best to start with some basic assets for which you have sufficient information to complete an assessment.

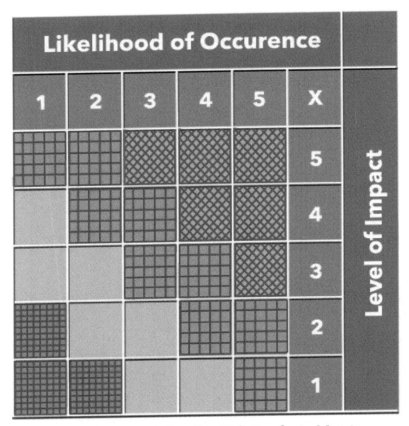

Figure C-1. Example of a Risk Analysis Matrix

Scenario #1

Assumptions:

- You have a website to conduct business with your customers, and it is hosted by a cloud services provider.
- Your website is the primary customer interface with your business.
- You and your staff maintain the actual website content.
- The cloud services provider manages the underlying web server and network connections.

- The cloud services provider applies the latest security patches and maintains several security measures to protect the server itself, with very limited vulnerabilities.
- You have an agreement with the cloud services provider for enhanced security services, so they ensure your web content and applications contain safety measures against abuse or unauthorized access.
- There is a potential for high impact to the business if something happens to the web site and it becomes unavailable.
- The cloud services provider performed a basic vulnerability assessment and found only a few known threats to your website (operating system, web site software, and infrastructure).

Based on this information, you would probably rate the asset's level of impact at 5, and the likelihood of occurrence at 2. So the overall website asset, in this scenario, would receive a risk rating of medium-high from the corresponding box in the matrix.

Scenario #2

Assumptions (we will use the basic information from Scenario #1 and apply a few changes):

- Now, the website is secondary to your customer interaction, with the primary means being in-person at your office.
- There has been a report issued from a third-party audit of the cloud services provider which has determined that they have not been diligent in their responsibilities for keeping the hosting environment secure; in particular, they have not kept fully current on security patches or fully protecting the web servers.
- The cloud services provider's lack of diligence in maintaining their hosting environment also impacted your website, and

the security of your web content and applications are in question.

- As a result of the third-party audit, the cloud services provider agreed to have vulnerability assessments done for all of its customers; results for your website show there are several known, active threats against the vulnerabilities that were found.

With these changes, let's say you now rate the level of impact at 3, and the likelihood of occurrence at 5, with a resulting risk rating of high.

Scenario #3

Assumptions (these are new and not based on the prior scenarios):

- You are using a stand-alone financial accounting software application, such as QuickBooks™, installed on a local computer in your office which is not connected to a network.
- This is the main purpose of the computer, so it cannot be used for internet surfing or email; it is connected to a printer for reports, and it gets backed up weekly on an external USB hard drive.
- You do not have automatic updates for the operating system, so you manually update security patches weekly; it has the latest anti-malware program, which is set to scan all portable and removable media as soon as they are connected to the computer, and you also manually update malware signatures weekly.
- The accounting application requires a unique user ID and a strong password (at least 12 characters with a mixture of upper-case and lower-case letters, numbers, and special characters) to log in and access your financial information, and access is limited to you and two other employees.

Based on these assumptions, you might rate the level of impact at 2 and, because the computer is isolated from any network and therefore threats are minimal, you might rate the likelihood of occurrence at 1. This results in an overall risk rating of low.

Depending on your risk tolerance, the first two scenarios could both be considered unacceptable risks, and appropriate actions should be taken to reduce the risk levels. This can be accomplished by a combination of eliminating vulnerabilities, mitigating the threats, and lowering the business impact. As part of your business risk management plan, you should address the principle of not having "all your eggs in one basket." This applies to all areas of the business, not just computer systems – you don't want a single point of failure that could completely shut down your business. Therefore, one strategy is to provide some redundancy in equipment and systems, so that if one fails, the alternate one can continue operating. This step alone can help mitigate risks and lower the business impact for a single asset. Realizing that redundancy can be costly, you would want to prioritize the high-risk assets and only provide redundancy for mission-critical assets. Keep in mind that these measures also apply to non-cyber risks (i.e., natural or man-made disasters), and would fit into a business continuity plan or disaster recovery plan.

As far as reducing vulnerabilities, if you are not able and don't have the skills to adequately configure security settings for a particular computer system, program, or network device, you should seek the assistance of a cybersecurity professional. Also, your Internet service provider may offer some assistance on how to configure the settings for their network device (modem or router). The basic requirement will be keeping the operating system up to date with the automatic update feature enabled, plus having local anti-malware programs on all computers, which are also automatically updated.

We've gone into some detail to help you gain a better understanding of the process for identifying and categorizing cyber risks. Now, let's bring this back up to the level of the risk management plan. The risk management plan should:

- identify the process methodology (refer back to chapter 4)
- identify what risk factors will be considered for each type of critical asset
- provide a statement about reaching an acceptable level of risk or using one of the other techniques for addressing each risk
- list cyber risk factors alongside other risk factors, where applicable

In the end, even with all of this risk information defined and documented, if your small business just doesn't have the expertise to perform an adequate risk assessment, then you need to hire a professional firm. Having your own risk management plan will go a long way in helping govern the work of an outside consultant, and potentially keep the cost of an assessment more under your control.

Appendix C – Key Points and Action Items

The following is a quick summary of the key points from this appendix:

- Each business should have a risk management plan which defines levels of acceptable risk, categorizes critical assets by risk level, and describes methods for addressing risk, with the goal of lowering overall business risk.

- Four primary techniques for handling risk include (1) eliminate the risk, (2) mitigate the risk, (3) transfer the risk, and (4) accept the risk.

- Risk factors fall into two general categories – internal risk factors, such as financial and workforce risk, and external risk factors, such as the regional economy and regulatory compliance.

- Cyber risk should be just another type of business operational risk and included in business risk assessments, especially when related to information assets.

- One common risk assessment uses a two-factor matrix that is based on the level of business impact and the likelihood of occurrence. Each critical asset should receive a risk level rating based on the analysis of these two factors for each asset.

- Using a risk evaluation matrix, such as a heat map, makes it easier for management to make informed cybersecurity decisions that incorporate the organization's risk tolerance level.

- A cyber risk assessment should be used as part of an overall business risk analysis and lowering cyber risk levels results in lower overall business risk.

- Where financially feasible, providing redundancy for critical computer systems can lower risk levels for both cyberattacks and other disasters.

Here are some simple actions you can take to start integrating cybersecurity risks into the risk management plan for your small business:

- Identify cyber risk as a category or type of business risk in the business plan or risk management plan. Include these risks in assessments and mitigation actions.
- Ensure that the risk management plan includes the organization's goals and techniques for addressing internal and external risks and defines acceptable risk levels for different types of assets.
- Ensure that there is a definition of what constitutes a critical asset and how they should be identified for risk assessments. Then, perform an inventory to identify all critical assets.
- Based on your industry sector and risk tolerance level, create a risk assessment matrix to use in assigning a risk value for each critical asset.
- Using a standard risk management methodology, determine whether identified risks for each critical asset will be eliminated, transferred, mitigated, or accepted.
- Include the results of any cyber risk assessment within an overall business risk analysis.

Appendix D

Document Templates and Examples

The documents described on the following pages are intended to help guide small businesses in developing a customized version of each type of document, specifically for your business. The templates provide an easy method for a small business to fill in some basic information, specific to the business, and have a finished document with minimal effort. The following documents are included in this Appendix:

1. Generic Business Plan, including a Risk Management Plan
2. Cybersecurity Strategy and Program Definition
3. Information Security Policy
4. IT Asset Inventory Worksheet
5. Cybersecurity Awareness and Training Policy
6. Cybersecurity Incident Response Plan

The descriptions of the templates in this Appendix are for your reference to help you select what will fit your business requirements. The actual templates are intended to be filled out using word processing software on an 8 1/2" x 11" page size. The Microsoft Word version of each template is available for download on the *CISO DRG* website at: https://cisodrg.com/project/creating-a-small-business-cybersecurity-program/ (scroll down to the bottom of the web page).

For the "Computer Security Incident Response Plan/Policy" template, you will find a short policy statement, then a checklist of action items that should occur before, during, and after an incident, along with a few forms to help capture information which might later aid in the investigation of an incident. There is a "short version" and a "comprehensive version" of the template available on the website above, that were created for organizations with 100-250 and 500+ employees, respectively. These additional templates contain greater detail, which a small business may or may not want to use.

DISCLAIMER: The templates are provided for informational purposes only, without any warranty of fitness for any particular purpose, business or industry, or of their applicability to any specific business circumstances and are not intended to be a substitute for professional advice. Your reliance on any information provided by the publisher, its affiliates, content providers, members, employees or comment contributors is solely at your own risk. This publication is sold with the understanding that the publisher is not engaged in rendering professional services. If advice or other expert assistance is required, the services of a competent professional person should be sought.

LICENSING NOTICE: The template documents, except for the Business Plan outline (which was derived from the SBA/SCORE), are provided on the *CISO DRG* website under the:

> Creative Commons Attribution-NonCommercial-ShareAlike 4.0 International license (CC BY-NC-SA 4.0)

> The license is available at https://creativecommons.org/licenses/by-nc-sa/4.0/legalcode.

(1) Generic Business Plan (Outline)

There are many examples of a Business Plan available from several sources, including free templates to help a business of almost any size create its own. The outline below is primarily following the guidelines from the U.S. Small Business Administration, from their resource partner, SCORE. The outline below may contain more information (subsections) than you would use for your small business, and it may not include some specific information that you would want to use. Small business owners are encouraged to contact the SBA/SCORE for assistance in creating a customized Business Plan.

There are also two templates available from SCORE:

- Business Plan Template for Established Business

    o https://www.score.org/resource/business-plan-template-established-business

- Business Plan Template for a Startup Business

    o https://www.score.org/resource/business-plan-template-startup-business

The Business Plan often starts with a non-disclosure (NDA) statement, because it contains confidential and proprietary information the business wants to protect. The outline of sections and topics follows the NDA and a disclaimer, as shown below:

Confidentiality and Non-Disclosure Agreement

The undersigned Reader acknowledges that this Business Plan for [Your Company Name] contains confidential and proprietary information, as well as information that is in the public domain. The Reader further acknowledges that any unauthorized disclosure of such confidential information may result in serious harm or damage to [Your Company Name] and, therefore, the undersigned Reader agrees not to disclose or use any information from this Business Plan without the express, prior written approval of [Legal Counsel or other executive manager].

Upon request, the undersigned Reader shall immediately return this Business Plan to [Name/Title of Position].

Signed: _____ ("Reader")

Print Name: _____

Date: _____

Disclaimer

This is a Business Plan and it does not imply any offering of securities.

Business Plan (Outline)

1.0   Executive Summary
2.0   General Business Description
    2.1   Mission Statement
    2.2   Goals and Objectives
    2.3   Business Philosophy
    2.4   Target Customers/Clients
    2.5   Description of Industry
    2.6   Strengths and Core Competencies
    2.7   Legal Form of Ownership
3.0   Products and Services
    3.1   Description of Services
    3.2   Factors Related to Competitive Advantage/Disadvantage
    3.3   Pricing and Rate Structure
4.0   Marketing Plan
    4.1   SWOT Analysis
    4.2   Competitor Data Collection
    4.3   Competitive Analysis
    4.4   Marketing Expenses Strategy
    4.5   Pricing Strategy
    4.6   Distribution Channel Assessment
5.0   Operational Plan
    5.1   Business Location
    5.2   Personnel and Staffing
    5.3   Legal Environment
    5.4   Accounts Receivable/Accounts Payable Policies
6.0   Management and Organization
    6.1   Management Worksheet
    6.2   Organization Chart
7.0   Startup Expenses and Capitalization
8.0   Financial Plan
    8.1   12-Month Profit/Loss Projection
    8.2   Projected Cash Flow

(2) Cybersecurity Strategy & Program Definition (Template)

This document template is used to create a strategic direction for how your small business intends to apply cybersecurity control measures through the creation of a cybersecurity program and implementing applicable policies and procedures. The cybersecurity program is defined as part of the strategy document; although, it could also be a separate document.

Specific wording within the template may be modified to suit the specific needs of your small business. In the area of "Roles and Responsibilities," remove the positions that are not part of your business structure and add others that you think should be included. It is not expected that a small business will have all of the separate staff positions identified in the template; however, it is important to assign the described functions and tasks to actual staffing positions. Below you will find the outline of sections and topics for the template.

Cybersecurity Strategy and Program Definition

1.0   Management Commitment
2.0   Purpose and Goals
3.0   Strategy Statement
4.0   Creation of a Cybersecurity Program
      4.1   Roles and Responsibilities
          Chief Executive Officer (CEO), President or Owner
          Chief Information Officer (CIO)
          Chief Information Security Officer (CISO), Chief
          Security Officer (CSO) or Information Security
          Manager
          Information Security Analyst/Specialist
          Network Administrator
          System Administrator
          Website Administrator
          Cyber Threat Intelligence Analyst
          Risk Assessment Specialist
          General End User
      4.2   Minimum Information Security Policies and
          Procedures (refer to the information security policy
          template below)
      4.3   Use of Standardized Security Controls
      4.4   Cybersecurity Awareness and Training Program

5.0   Emergency Management Planning for Information Security
      5.1   Business Continuity Plan
      5.2   Disaster Recovery Plan
6.0   Cybersecurity Incident Response Plan
7.0   Regular Review of Cybersecurity Strategy and Cybersecurity
      Program

(3) Information Security Policy (Template)

A good method for keeping track of policies is to have a header block which identifies the policy, usually with a policy number and title, version number, the effective date, sometimes page numbering, and who authorized or approved it. In some cases, there is also a target date for its review and re-approval; although this might simply be stated within the policy itself. The heading block is usually repeated as a page header. It should be noted that if you plan to create a series of separate policies for the different topics, you should start with the shell of the online template, maintain the header block, and be sure to copy or include a Purpose, Scope, and Definitions for each policy. The policy template is a single document with separate sections for each topic.

Information Security Policy

1.0	Purpose
2.0	Scope
3.0	Definitions
4.0	User account management policy
5.0	Internet and email acceptable use policy
6.0	Sensitive and confidential information policy
7.0	Wireless access and remote access policy
8.0	Virtual private network (vpn) and encryption policy
9.0	Software updates and patch management policy
10.0	Portable and mobile device security policy
11.0	System administration security policy
12.0	Third-party access policy
13.0	Identity theft awareness training policy
14.0	Related security standards and procedures
15.0	Penalties

(4) IT Asset Inventory Worksheet (Template)

The small-scale version of this worksheet below provides you with the information you should be collecting on each information asset. Having this worksheet available for physical inventories will facilitate data entry and updates to an automated asset management system. You will use one form for each asset, so you should plan on having a laptop or notepad computer with the template installed, then as you complete the physical inventory of each asset, save the file using the asset ID as the filename.

The physical inventory should include comparing what devices you find with (a) the company's purchase records for the first time through the process, and (b) devices identified during a previous, automated asset discovery process. The purchase information should be entered into the last few boxes on the form. You only need to complete the sections and boxes of the inventory form that apply to each asset, leaving the rest blank.

For the Asset ID, you should create something that makes sense to you within your business environment. You should be able to use a combination of letters and numbers, with a maximum of 32 or 64 characters, depending on the system being used. Many companies use an alphabetic prefix representing the company name (three to eight letters), followed by a sequential number (four or five digits), so that each new asset receives the next higher number in the sequence. You may use the asset inventory sheet at the end of this appendix.

(5) Cybersecurity Awareness and Training Policy (Template)

First, we provide a checklist below of nine items to be included in a basic cybersecurity awareness and training program for a small business with less than 50 employees. Second, the online template provides a more detailed program for organizations with 50-500 employees. The template may contain sections that do not apply to your small business. However, you may decide to include some additional provisions from the template to the checklist as you customize the plan for your small business.

To create a simplified cybersecurity awareness and training program for your small business, you can extract the following nine sections from the template and customize them to meet your needs. The intent is to reduce the complexity and scope of the original template into an easily manageable policy. Where applicable in the checklist below, you will see indicators for the CIS Sub-Control that is being met by a particular section of the policy.

1. Purpose and Goal Statement: management's reason for having the policy and the business goal(s) they hope to achieve.

2. Scope: who must follow the policy and to what extent is the training conducted internally versus externally through a training contractor.

3. Policy Statement: briefly define the requirements and expectations. [CIS Sub-Control 17.3]

4. Definitions: optional, but recommended to include at least some basic terminology.

5. Responsibilities: only include the relevant positions for your business.

6. Awareness Program: define the topics to be covered, the methods of delivery, and the frequency of distribution or presentation.

7. Employee Training: describe any mandatory training courses, when they must be completed, and the frequency of any refresher courses. The following topics should be considered mandatory, to meet the requirements of the CIS Controls.

> (a)   Secure authentication [CIS Sub-Control 17.5]
> (b)   Identifying social engineering attacks [CIS Sub-Control 17.6]
> (c)   Sensitive data handling [CIS Sub-Control 17.7]
> (d)   Causes of unintentional data exposure [CIS Sub-Control 17.8]
> (e)   Identifying and reporting cybersecurity incidents [CIS Sub-Control 17.9]

8. Awareness and Training for Non-Employees: describe the requirements for any third-party contractors, consultants, vendors, suppliers or other non-employees who will have access to your business computer systems, if applicable.

9. Evaluation of Awareness and Training Program: optional, but recommended – define the requirements to review and evaluate the effectiveness of the program, including costs, usually on an annual basis to align with the business budget cycle.

Below is the outline for the template:

CYBERSECURITY AWARENESS & TRAINING POLICY

1.0	Background and Purpose.
2.0	Scope.
3.0	Policy.
4.0	Definitions.
5.0	Responsibilities.
	5.1 Content-Related Responsibilities:
	5.2 Position-Related Responsibilities:
6.0	Cybersecurity Awareness Program.
7.0	Cybersecurity Training for Employees.
	7.1 New Employee Training Requirements:
	7.2 Ongoing Training Requirements:
8.0	Cybersecurity Training for Non-Employees.
	8.1 Initial Training for Non-Employees:
	8.2 Ongoing or Additional Training for Non-Employees:
9.0	Evaluation & Review of Cybersecurity Awareness & Training Program.
10.0	External Awareness & Training Resources.

The following government and non-profit web sites offer cybersecurity awareness resources (mostly free), ranging from general information to tips for protection against specific types of cybercrimes, such as identity theft. Some places offer training (for a fee).

- Stay Safe Online (National Cybersecurity Alliance)

  o http://www.staysafeonline.org/

- On Guard Online (U.S. Department of Homeland Security)

  o http://www.onguardonline.gov/
  o Videos/Games: http://www.onguardonline.gov/media

- Stop. Think. Connect. Campaign (private-public collaboration)

  o http://www.stopthinkconnect.org/

- State of California, Office of Information Security (videos)

  o http://cio.ca.gov/OIS/Government/video/default.asp

- Multi-State Information Sharing & Analysis Center, Training Resources (MS-ISAC, Center for Internet Security)

  o http://msisac.cisecurity.org/resources/videos/

- Identity Theft Resource Center (non-profit organization)

  o http://www.idtheftcenter.org/

- SANS Institute, Security Resources

  o http://www.sans.org/security-resources/

(6) Cyber Security Incident Response Plan (Small Business Template)

The incident response plan template, along with the action items and tracking forms, is meant to provide a small business (less than 50 employees) with just the basic needs for responding to a cybersecurity incident. There are two additional templates available on the *CISO DRG* website, one "Shortened, Condensed" version for businesses with 50-500 employees, and one "Comprehensive" version for organizations with 500+ employees. Review those templates to determine if there is additional information you want to include in your incident response plan, beyond what is included in the following template.

Cyber Security Incident Response Plan

Statement of Management Commitment
Mission & Goals for Incident Response
Senior Management Approval of Plan
   Document Revision History
Policy
Purpose & Objectives of the Plan
Scope
Definitions
Cyber Security Incident Response Roles
Considerations Before, During, and After a Cybersecurity Incident
Planning and Preparation
Communications
Interaction with other organizations
External Information Sharing
Coordination with law enforcement
Collection and preservation of evidence
Reporting requirements
Security Incident Management Lifecycle
Incident Response Management – Glossary of Terms

Incident Communications Tracking Template
Incident Handling Checklist
Detailed Incident Handling Checklist/Template

Incident Response Management References and Resources

The following list of documents provides detailed information on different aspects of computer security incident management and response. These documents provide valuable resources for management to identify best practices for risk management and incident response. The also allow for Incident Response Team members to learn about different aspects of security protective and responsive measures. [*Author's Note: the hyperlink for each document was valid at the time of publication; however, there is a possibility that some have changed. You can go to the NIST website at **https://csrc.nist.gov/** and search for the topic or title.*]

- NIST Information Technology Laboratory (ITL) Bulletin, September 2012, *Handling Security-Related Incidents* (overview of NIST Special Publication 800-61, Rev. 2)

  o http://csrc.nist.gov/publications/nistbul/itlbul2012_09.pdf

- NIST Special Publication SP-800-37, Rev. 2, Dec. 2018, *Guide for Applying the Risk Management Framework to Federal Information Systems*

  o https://doi.org/10.6028/NIST.SP.800-37r2

- NIST Special Publication SP-800-61, Rev. 2, Aug. 2012, *Computer Security Incident Handling Guide*

  o https://doi.org/10.6028/NIST.SP.800-61r2

- NIST Special Publication SP-800-83, Rev. 1, July 2013, Guide to Malware Incident Prevention and Handling for Desktops and Laptops

  o https://doi.org/10.6028/NIST.SP.800-83r1

- NIST Special Publication SP-800-86, Sept. 2006, Guide to Integrating Forensic Techniques into Incident Response

- https://doi.org/10.6028/NIST.SP.800-86

- NIST Special Publication SP-800-92, Sept. 2006 *Guide to Computer Security Log Management*

  - https://doi.org/10.6028/NIST.SP.800-92

- NIST Special Publication SP-800-94, Feb. 2007, *Guide to Intrusion Detection and Prevention Systems (IDS/IPS)*

  - https://doi.org/10.6028/NIST.SP.800-94

- NIST Special Publication SP-800-128, Aug. 2011, *Guide for Security-Focused Configuration Management of Information Systems*

  - https://doi.org/10.6028/NIST.SP.800-128

- NIST Special Publication SP-800-137, Sept. 2011, *Information Security Continuous Monitoring (ISCM)*

  - https://doi.org/10.6028/NIST.SP.800-137

- NIST Special Publication SP-800-150, Oct. 2016, *Guide to Cyber Threat Information Sharing*

  - https://doi.org/10.6028/NIST.SP.800-150

- Software Engineering Institute, CERT Program, Carnegie-Mellon University, "*Incident Management Capability Assessment*", Dec. 2018

  - https://resources.sei.cmu.edu/asset_files/TechnicalRepo rt/2018_005_001_538866.pdf

The following organization web sites and resource document links are provided as reference information, in addition to the documents listed above, on the topic of computer security-related Incident Management and its components. These sources may benefit Incident Response Team members in learning more about their roles and responsibilities and provide managers and executives a better understanding of the interconnected relationships between business risk, cybersecurity, and incident management.

(A) Organizations

- U.S. Department of Homeland Security, National Cybersecurity Division, U.S. Computer Emergency Readiness Team (US-CERT)

    o https://www.us-cert.gov/

- CERT Coordination Center, Carnegie Mellon University

    o http://www.cert.org/incident-management/

- National Institute of Standards & Technology (NIST), Computer Security Resource Center

    o http://csrc.nist.gov/

- Information Systems Audit and Control Association (ISACA)

    o https://www.isaca.org/

- Center for Internet Security, Multi-State Information Sharing & Analysis Center (MS-ISAC)

    o http://msisac.cisecurity.org/

- InfraGard National Members Alliance

    o http://infragardmembers.org

- Information Systems Security Association (ISSA)

    o https://www.issa.org/

(B) Incident Management Documents

- Action List for Developing a Computer Security Incident Response Team, August 2014, CERT/CC

- o http://www.cert.org/incident-management/csirt-development/action-list.cfm

- Combating the Insider Threat, May 2014, US-CERT

  - o https://www.us-cert.gov/sites/default/files/publications/Combating%20the%20Insider%20Threat_0.pdf

- Creating a Computer Security Incident Response Team: A Process for Getting Started, August 2014, CERT/CC

  - o http://www.cert.org/incident-management/products-services/creating-a-csirt.cfm

- Defining Incident Management Processes for CSIRTs: A Work in Progress, October 2004, SEI

  - o http://resources.sei.cmu.edu/asset_files/TechnicalReport/2004_005_001_14405.pdf

- Handbook for Computer Security Incident Response Teams (CSIRTs), 2nd Edition, April 2003, SEI

  - o http://resources.sei.cmu.edu/asset_files/Handbook/2003_002_001_14102.pdf

- Incident Management (Whitepaper), December 2005, CERT/CC

  - o http://resources.sei.cmu.edu/asset_files/WhitePaper/2005_019_001_295923.pdf

- Malware Threats and Mitigation Strategies, May 2005, US-CERT & MS-ISAC

  - o https://www.us-cert.gov/sites/default/files/publications/malware-threats-mitigation.pdf

- Staffing Your Computer Security Incident Response Team – What Basic Skills are Needed, August 2014, CERT/CC

  o http://www.cert.org/incident-management/csirt-development/csirt-staffing.cfm

Inventory Date	
Completed By	
Assigned Asset ID	
Type of Asset	☐ Desktop/Tower ☐ Laptop ☐ Tablet ☐ Smartphone ☐ Printer ☐ Multi-Function Device (Print/Scan/Fax/Copy) ☐ Network Wired Router ☐ Network Wireless Router Other (specify): _____
Asset Primary Purpose	
Manufacturer & Model	
Serial Number	
MAC Address(es)	____ : ____ : ____ : ____ : ____ : ____

Processor(s) [CPUs]	#1 Manufacturer/Type/Speed: _____
	  ☐ Dual Processor ☐ Quad Processor
	
	#2 Manufacturer/Type/Speed: _____
	  ☐ Dual Processor ☐ Quad Processor

Memory [RAM]	_____ GB
Operating System	☐ Windows-Version/Release # ☐ Mac OS- Version/Release # ☐ Linux-Distribution Name/Version: _____ ☐ Other (specify): _____
Internal Disk Drive(s)	#1 Capacity_____ GB / TB (circle one) #2 Capacity_____ GB / TB (circle one) #3 Capacity_____ GB / TB (circle one)
External Disk Drive(s)	#1 Capacity_____ GB / TB (circle one) #2 Capacity_____ GB / TB (circle one)
Internal Optical Drive(s)	☐ CD Drive ☐ CD R-Drive ☐ CD-RW Drive ☐ DVD Drive ☐ DVDR-Drive ☐ DVD-RW Drive ☐ Blu- Ray Drive ☐ Other (specify)

Inventory Asset Form 1 of 2

Display Monitor(s)	#1 Manufacturer & Model
	   Serial # _____
	#2 Manufacturer & Model
	   Serial # _____

Associated Peripheral Device(s)	☐ Dedicated Printer – Serial # _____
	   Manufacturer/Model _____
	
	☐ Specify Device #2 _____
	   Manufacturer/Model _____
	   Serial # _____
	
	☐ Specify Device #3 _____
	   Manufacturer/Model _____
	   Serial # _____

Date Placed in Service	
Assigned User	
Assigned Location	
Internal IP Address	_____ . _____ . _____ . _____
Assigned Group(s)	

Assigned Software Licenses	#1 Title/Version_____
	   License Key _____
	#2 Title/Version_____
	   License Key _____
	#3 Title/Version_____
	   License Key _____
	#4 Title/Version_____
	   License Key _____
	#5 Title/Version_____
	   License Key _____

Hardware Support Contract	
Software Support Contract	
Purchase Date	
Purchase Cost	
Purchased From	

Inventory Asset Form 2 of 2

Index

Index

Alan Watkins is a Core Adjunct Professor for the Cybersecurity and Information Assurance MS/BS degree programs at National University, teaching online courses since 2012. He was an independent cybersecurity consultant from 2011 to 2019, where his focus was public awareness of cybersecurity and identity theft prevention, as well as assisting small businesses. He has a Bachelor of Science Degree in Management and a Master of Science Degree in Business Administration, both from San Diego State University. Alan has 40 years of experience in the field of information technology and 20 years of experience in the field of cybersecurity, along with 10 years in emergency management and 12 years in law enforcement. He has been a member of InfraGard San Diego since it formed in 2005 and has 18 years of experience with critical infrastructure protection, which includes industrial control systems (ICS) and supervisory control and data acquisition (SCADA) systems.

Alan was the primary contributor and lead editor on a booklet for small businesses, created and distributed by the non-profit, Securing Our eCITY Foundation in San Diego. The book, *Bringing IT Home – Critical Infrastructure for Small Businesses: Prepare, Prevent, Respond, and Recover*, provides real-world examples of threats to small businesses for each of the 18 critical infrastructure sectors, along with actions they can take to prepare in advance of an incident, help prevent incidents, how to respond to an incident, and how to recover from an incident.

LinkedIn Profile:
    https://www.linkedin.com/in/alan-watkins-9203b630

Made in the USA
Middletown, DE
09 May 2022

65353233R00141